W0245737

Whitestein Series in Software Agent Technologies

Series Editors:
Marius Walliser
Stefan Brantschen
Monique Calisti
Thomas Hempfling

This series reports new developments in agent-based software technologies and agent-oriented software engineering methodologies, with particular emphasis on applications in various scientific and industrial areas. It includes research level monographs, polished notes arising from research and industrial projects, outstanding PhD theses, and proceedings of focused meetings and conferences. The series aims at promoting advanced research as well as at facilitating know-how transfer to industrial use.

About Whitestein Technologies

Whitestein Technologies AG was founded in 1999 with the mission to become a leading provider of advanced software agent technologies, products, solutions, and services for various applications and industries. Whitestein Technologies strongly believes that software agent technologies, in combination with other leading-edge technologies like web services and mobile wireless computing, will enable attractive opportunities for the design and the implementation of a new generation of distributed information systems and network infrastructures.

www.whitestein.com

Manuel Günter

Customer-based
IP Service Monitoring
with Mobile
Software Agents

Springer Basel AG

Author's e-mail address:
manuel.guenter@iname.com

2000 Mathematical Subject Classification 68U35, 68T35, 94A99

A CIP catalogue record for this book is available from the
Library of Congress, Washington D.C., USA

Deutsche Bibliothek Cataloging-in-Publication Data
Günter, Manuel:
Customer based IP service monitoring with mobile software agents /
Manuel Günter. - Basel ; Boston ; Berlin : Birkhäuser, 2002
   (Whitestein series in software agent technologies)
   ISBN 978-3-7643-6917-0   ISBN 978-3-0348-8185-2 (eBook)
   DOI 10.1007/978-3-0348-8185-2

ISBN 978-3-7643-6917-0

This work is subject to copyright. All rights are reserved, whether the whole or part of the material is concerned, specifically the rights of translation, reprinting, re-use of illustrations, recitation,
broadcasting, reproduction on microfilms or in other ways, and storage in data banks. For any kind
of use permission of the copyright owner must be obtained.

© 2002 Springer Basel AG
Originally published by Birkhäuser Verlag in 2002

Cover design: Micha Lotrovsky, CH-4106 Therwil, Switzerland
Printed on acid-free paper produced from chlorine-free pulp. TCF ∞

ISBN 978-3-7643-6917-0

9 8 7 6 5 4 3 2 1   www.birkhauser-science.com

Contents

Abstract   ix

Preface   xi

1 Introduction   1
   1.1 Overall Scenario   2
   1.2 Advanced IP Network Services   2
        1.2.1 Internet-based Virtual Private Network (VPN)   3
        1.2.2 The Security Architecture for the Internet Protocol . . .   5
        1.2.3 Differentiated Services (DiffServ)   10
   1.3 Agent Technology   11
   1.4 Network and Service Management   12
   1.5 The Problem and the Proposed Approach   14
   1.6 Outline of the Book   14

2 A Service Monitoring Architecture   17
   2.1 Introduction and Motivation   17
   2.2 Mobility and Service Monitoring   19
        2.2.1 Terminology   19
        2.2.2 Advantages of Service Monitoring with Mobile Agents . . . 20
   2.3 The Basic Infrastructure   21
        2.3.1 Location of the Control Points   21
        2.3.2 Node Architecture   22
        2.3.3 Authorization and Filtering   24
        2.3.4 Security Issues   25
   2.4 Mobility Models and Agent Forwarding   25
        2.4.1 Supported Mobility Models   25
        2.4.2 Forwarding Security   26
   2.5 Internet Deployment   27
        2.5.1 Advanced Infrastructure Support   27

3 Implementation of CSM   29
   3.1 The CSM Protocol   31
        3.1.1 Overview   31
        3.1.2 Internet Communication with Java   31
        3.1.3 Layering of the CSM Protocol   33
        3.1.4 The Protocol Object   33
        3.1.5 Message Objects   34
        3.1.6 CSM Message Exchange Sequences   37
   3.2 The T-Component and the Raw Packet Protocol   37
        3.2.1 T-Component Implementations   39

3.2.2   The Interaction between the Node and the T-component   39

3.2.3   Other Options for T-components   41

3.3   The CSM Node   41

3.3.1   Node Overview   42

3.3.2   Welcome Procedure for an Agent   42

3.3.3   The Execution Environment   44

3.3.4   Node Services   45

3.3.5   User Profiles and Policies   49

3.4   Agent Interface   51

3.5   Security and Resource Control   53

3.5.1   Communication Protection   53

3.5.2   Security Layers of the Node   53

3.5.3   Resource Control   54

3.5.4   Agent Security   56

3.6   The Home Application   56

3.6.1   Implementation Overview   57

3.6.2   The Transmission of a Request to the Node   58

3.6.3   The Callback Displayer   60

3.6.4   Generic Views of the Agent Results   62

3.7   CSM Internetworking Support   63

3.7.1   Name and Topology Information   65

3.7.2   Routing   66

3.8   Organization of the Source Code   67

4   Applications of Service Monitoring Agents   69

4.1   Monitoring a Virtual Private Network Service   69

4.1.1   Functionality of a VPN Control Agent   70

4.1.2   Statistical Tests on Cryptographic Algorithms   72

4.2   Service Level Agreement Monitoring   77

4.3   Agents for Measuring QoS Parameters   79

4.3.1   Throughput Measurements   79

4.3.2   Coordination of Distributed Measurements   83

4.3.3   One-Way Delay Measurements   84

4.3.4   The Ping Measurements   86

4.4   Agent Security   91

4.4.1   Classification of Attacks   94

4.4.2   The Semantics of the Agent   95

4.4.3   Attacks on the Input of the Agent   98

4.4.4   Evaluation of the Threat Situation   99

4.5   Extended Application Scenarios 100

4.5.1   Further Applications Independent of New Node Services 100

4.5.2   Future CSM Extensions   102

5 Performance Evaluation **105**
5.1 Performance of the Node Environment 105
    5.1.1 Throughput of the Execution Environment 106
    5.1.2 Node Throughput Including the TCP Receiver 112
5.2 Agent Performance 113
5.3 Communication Performance of the CSM System 113
5.4 The T-Component 119
5.5 Discussion and Improvements 121

6 Comparison with Related Work **123**
6.1 The Internet2 Initiative and the QBone 123
    6.1.1 The QBone 124
    6.1.2 QBone Measurements 124
    6.1.3 Comparison to our Approach 125
6.2 Network Measurements and Monitoring 125
    6.2.1 IP Measurement Methodology 126
    6.2.2 The Simple Network Management Architecture 127
    6.2.3 Measurement Testbeds 130
6.3 Mobile Agents for Management and Monitoring 132
    6.3.1 Network Management with Mobile Agents 132
    6.3.2 The Script MIB 133
    6.3.3 Network Management with Active Networks 134
6.4 Open Issues 135
    6.4.1 Collaboration of Monitoring Agents 135
    6.4.2 Routing 136
    6.4.3 Artificial Intelligence 136

7 Summary and Conclusion **137**

List of Figures **143**

List of Tables **145**

List of Abbreviations **147**

Bibliography **151**

Abstract

Enhanced Internet services such as virtual private networks and high priority traffic offer new revenues for the struggling Internet service provider industry. Yet, for the commercial success of such IP services it is critical that the customer can immediately 'look & feel' their enhancement. Traditionally, a service provider generates monthly reports for the customers. This is insufficient for value-added IP services, since such reports are too coarse-grained, too easy to manipulate, and may not reflect the properties that the customer is interested in (e.g. security).

Mobile software agents can roam a computer network and autonomously fulfill a user-defined task. This book proposes a Customer-based Service Monitoring system (CSM) that exploits the unique ability of mobile agents. The customers of a value-added IP service can send out monitoring agents that verify the proper service operation and visualize and quantify the service enhancement. The mobile agents can carry out customer-defined service tests. The agents' main advantage is that they can perform the tests at the locations where the IP services are delivered: in the provider networks. Of course, this book discusses in detail how the CSM system must be designed to prevent abuses such as sniffing of other customers' traffic or denial-of-service attacks.

This book motivates the use of mobile software agents for service monitoring. It presents an architecture and an implementation of a CSM infrastructure. The book also introduces examples of enhanced IP services and of agents that monitor these services in new and innovative ways. Also, various performance issues are studied.

The work presented in this book is an excerpt from the Ph.D. thesis *Management of Multi-Provider Internet Services with Software Agents*, which was published in July, 2001. The thesis and CSM source code is available on the following URL: http://www.iam.unibe.ch/~mguenter/phd.html.

Preface

The following work was performed during my employment as research and lecture assistant at the Institute for Computer Science and Applied Mathematics (IAM) of the University of Bern, Switzerland. It is a revised version of a fundamental part of my PhD thesis (of which the complete version can be found in: [Gün01]). I would like to thank Prof. Dr. Torsten Braun, head of the Computer Network and Distributed Systems group (RVS), for supervising this work and for his insightful advice. I would also like to thank Prof. Dr. Burkhard Stiller, who revised the technical contents of this work, and Ms. Isabelle Huber, who revised the work's language. Many thanks go to my colleagues of the IAM institute and of the 'Advanced Network and Agent Infrastructure for the Support of Federations Of Workflow Trading Systems' (ANAISOFT) project. This project of the Swiss National Science Foundation (SNF) funded most of the work that I describe in this book.

Last but not least, I would like to thank my family and my friend Monika, who supported me throughout my studies.

Manuel Günter

Preface

The following work was performed during my case...

Chapter 1

Introduction

The Internet service providers are eager to create new and enhanced Internet Protocol (IP) services in order to support advanced network applications and to create new revenues. IP services may, for example, be enhanced by traffic prioritization and security guarantees. Yet, for Internet-wide service coverage IP services depend on the collaboration of several providers. Such multi-provider services profit from the economy of scale and attract more potential users. Ideally, such services span the whole Internet so that they can support a broader range of applications. However, today there is no service management platform for advanced multi-provider IP services available.

An important aspect of the service management is the *monitoring* of the services. Today, the providers try to hinder external insight into their network management out of security reasons. The customer of an enhanced network service is also denied insight. Nevertheless, the customer should be able to verify the enhancement of the service. For example, customers will not buy a secure network service if they cannot verify that the providers are really securing the service. The customer needs a way to verify that the IP service is indeed enhanced. Otherwise the customer will not pay the additional service charges. In case the service is provided through collaboration of multiple providers, they themselves may want to monitor if all partners collaborate as negotiated. This book presents a non-intrusive and generic customer-based service monitoring infrastructure (CSM). The proposed infrastructure exploits the unique ability of mobile software agents. The agents can roam to the network devices where the IP service is being delivered and thus monitor the service efficiently. Customers can use CSM to build up trust in the enhancement of their services. Providers can advertise the advantages of their service with CSM and can ensure collaboration among several providers in the case of multi-provider IP services.

The rest of this chapter introduces terminology and presents the state of the art of relevant technology. Section 1.1 describes the overall scenario. Section 1.2 presents two prominent examples of enhanced IP services: differentiated services and virtual private IP networks. Throughout this book these services are used as motivating examples. We propose to deploy agent technology to solve multi-provider service monitoring problems.

The state of the art in agent technology is described in section 1.3. Section 1.4 gives an overview of a widely used management reference model which is relevant to IP services, too. Given that introductory information, we will be able to restate the problems addressed in this book in more detail (see section 1.5). Section 1.6 outlines the book.

1.1   Overall Scenario

This book refers to an Internet model with actors, roles, and relations as depicted in figure 1.1. There are business entities called Internet service providers (ISP) selling IP services to customers. The business relation between customer and provider concerning this service is specified in a Service Level Agreement (SLA). This is a contract that describes the scope of delivery of the service in question. The SLA may be a traditional paper contract or an electronic contract. ISPs control an IP infrastructure in order to be able to provide Internet services. They may own network infrastructure or buy network services from other providers. Some Internet services, such as priority traffic services, require the collaboration of the involved ISPs. Throughout this book this topic is of interest because multi-provider collaboration is an open issue in many areas of Internet research.

The collaboration between providers is also regulated by service level agreements. Sometimes, one provider plays the role of the customer and sometimes both contracting parties play a symmetric provider role (peering agreements). Nevertheless, the SLAs between providers also describe what actions each party takes and what resources the parties devote to the deployment of the service. Thus, in many cases it is not necessary to distinguish between these different types of SLAs.

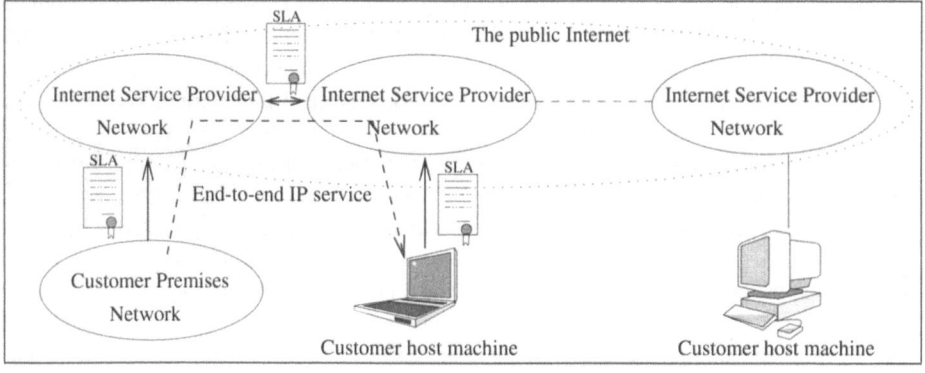

Figure 1.1: Overall scenario.

1.2   Advanced IP Network Services

The Internet technology introduced a new philosophy into the telecommunication world: the philosophy of the 'stupid' best-effort network [Ise97]. Such a network implements only a simple packet forwarding service without additional intelligence. Advanced services must be implemented in end devices (computers). Furthermore, the network capacity is shared. All packets are forwarded equally and as quickly as possible (best-effort). The rapid growth of the Internet reflects the success of this philosophy. Now the Internet is globally present and commercialized. Internet end-users try to handle as many telecommunication tasks as possible with the inexpensive Internet. However, some networking applications demand service quality; for example, IP telephony applications impose upper limits on network delays and delay jitter. Financial applications require communication privacy, whereas real-time video transmission needs bandwidth guarantees. The deployment of service quality in the Internet requires control mechanisms in the network, which therefore forces the Internet to become smarter. Service providers can deploy such intelligent mechanisms and use them to offer quality enhanced Internet services. This section describes two new and emerging Internet services: a virtual private network service and a quality-of-service related service differentiation. Throughout the book these two enhanced services serve as motivating examples.

1.2.1 Internet-based Virtual Private Network (VPN)

Large corporations used to interconnect local headquarters and branch offices with leased lines provided by telecommunication companies. They ran private networks, so-called corporate networks. With the rise of the Internet technology more and more corporate networks switched from various networking protocols (such as Novell) to the TCP/IP protocol suite. Such private networks based on the Internet technology are also referred to as Intranets. Since leased lines are expensive and the corporations often already have Internet connectivity, there is an economic pressure to replace the expensive leased lines and use the wide area interconnectivity of the global Internet instead. However, there are two problems that must be addressed: (1) The Intranet may use private addresses that are not unique in the global Internet and thus not routable [RMK+96]. (2) The Internet protocol does not assure privacy of transmission. While the IP packets travel through the public Internet, they may be eavesdropped or even altered. Virtual private networks [FH98a, FH98b, GHAM00] encapsulate the packets with private addresses into packets with public addresses. This process is referred to as *tunneling*. If privacy and authenticity of the encapsulated packet is desired, then this can be ensured with cryptographic means. Internet-based VPNs encapsulate IP packets in new IP packets.

Figure 1.2 shows the two most prominent VPN types: subnet-to-subnet VPNs and access VPNs.

- The subnet-to-subnet VPN interconnects geographically distributed private IP subnets. All traffic leaving one subnet destined for another is tunneled through the public Internet.

- The access VPN allows roaming users to dial into the virtual privat network from their home machines or from arbitrary Internet points-of-presence.

Figure 1.2 also illustrates the tunneling mechanism. It shows the structure of a tunneled IP packet originating from an application that runs within the private subnet X. The packet's destination is a machine in a remotely located part of the VPN (the private subnet Y). The subnets X and Y use private IP addresses which are not routed in the public Internet. The address structure of the VPN is invisible from the outside. The access routers of subnets X and Y incorporate VPN functionality. They have an interior network interface with a private IP address and an exterior network interface with a public IP address. The access router at X recognizes that the packet in question must be tunneled. It knows the public interface of the access router of subnet Y. It uses that address as destination address and its own public address as source address. The access router (also referred to as tunnel endpoint) creates a new IP packet with these new addresses and puts the original packet in the payload of the new packet. The payload is then encrypted. The new packet is sent to the tunnel endpoint at Y. The router there extracts the payload of the packet and decrypts the contents. So, the original packet is restored and can be routed on the private subnet Y towards the originally intended destination. The access VPN case also uses tunnels. However, there are two distinct possibilities. Either the home PC acts as a tunnel endpoint or else the point-of-presence (POP) of an ISP functions as tunnel endpoint.

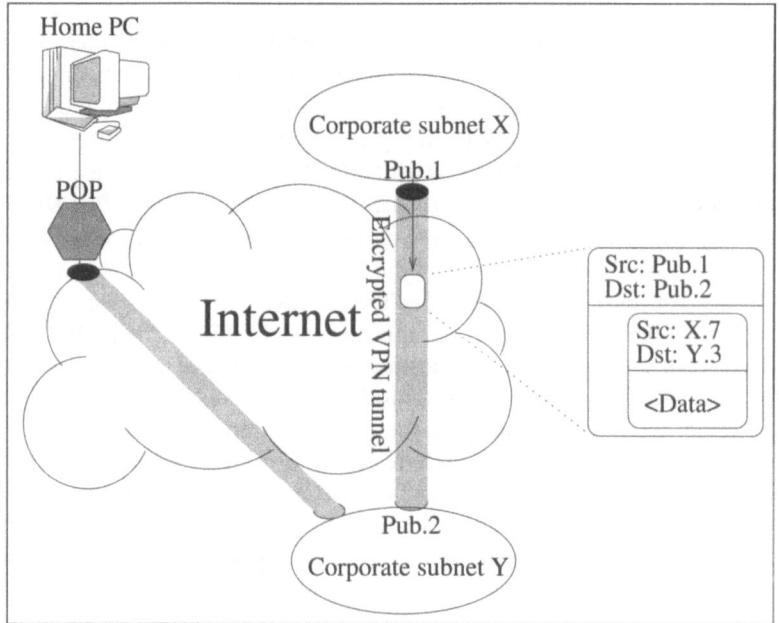

Figure 1.2: Virtual private network types.

The address translation between private and public networks and the involved routing and cryptographic mechanisms make virtual private networks hard to manage. While a VPN may be useful for a small-to-medium size company, the management of the VPN would require additional equipment and personnel. For this reason, there is a market for

VPN services that enables the customers to outsource the management of their VPN. The Internet service provider can deploy VPN capable border routers and use them to introduce a VPN on-demand service [KBG00]. So several VPNs can be managed on the same infrastructure by the same personnel (of the ISP); thus both the customer and the provider can profit from the economy of scale.

1.2.2 The Security Architecture for the Internet Protocol

The Internet Engineering Task Force (IETF) standardized IP version 6 (IPv6) [DH98] to solve pending problems (such as address shortage) of the current version of the IP protocol (IPv4). A spin-off development of this process was the IP security architecture (IPSec) which introduces per-packet security features. While the IP version 6 deployment has been delayed, the security architecture has been adopted in the current IP version (IPv4). A key motivation for this was that IPSec includes all mechanisms needed to implement VPNs.

The Internet security architecture comprises a family of protocols. IPSec describes IP packet header extensions and packet trailers that provide security features. The per-packet security features come from two protocols: the Authentication Header (AH) [KA98a] that provides packet integrity as well as authenticity and the Encapsulating Security Payload (ESP) [KA98b] creating privacy through encryption. AH and ESP are independent protocols that can be used separately and that can be concatenated. One reason for the separation was that there are countries that have restrictive regulations on encrypted communication. There, IPSec can be deployed solely using AH because authentication mechanisms are not regulated.

Both ESP and AH have two modi: the transport mode and the tunnel mode. The transport mode extends the IP headers by adding new fields. The tunnel mode adds a completely new IP header (plus extension fields). The transport mode allows the user to run IPSec end-to-end. The tunnel mode is ideal for implementing a VPN tunnel at Internet access routers (see figure 1.2). In tunnel mode both AH and ESP can be used to implement IP-VPN tunnels. AH and ESP dispose of a small standardized set of cryptographic algorithms to ensure authenticity and privacy. This set is required in order to guarantee interoperability between different IPSec implementations. Beside of that both protocols are specified independent of cryptographic algorithms. A new encryption algorithm, for example, can easily be added to IPSec. Both AH and ESP assume the presence of a secret key. This key material may be installed manually. A better and more scalable approach is to use the third protocol of the IPSec family: the Internet Key Exchange protocol (IKE) [HC98].

At some point in the network both AH and ESP perform a transformation to IP packets. The IPSec compliant machines always form sender-receiver pairs where the sender performs the transformation and the receiver reverses it. The relation between sender and receiver is described as a *security association*. Note that the security association defines just one transformation (and its inverse). Concatenated AH and ESP transformations are described by concatenated security associations which can be regarded as descriptions of 'open' IPSec connections. Both IPSec peering machines store representations of security associations. The representations include information about what kind of protocol is used (AH or ESP) in what mode, what kind of cryptographic algorithms as well as the secret key that are used. Each IPSec compliant machine may be involved in an arbitrary number of security associations that are identified by a 32-bit number, the so-called *Security Parameter Index* (SPI). The sending party writes the SPI into the appropriate field of the IP protocol extension, whereas the receiver uses this information to identify the correct security association. In that way the receiver is able to invert the transformation and to restore the original packet. Let us have a closer look at the IPSec protocols and their security features.

The Encapsulation Security Payload

The Internet Assigned Numbers Authority (IANA) has assigned the protocol number 50 for the IPSec encapsulation security payload. ESP ensures privacy of the IP payload. For that purpose an ESP header and an ESP trailer clamp the IP payload between them. The payload and the trailer are encrypted. The ESP also provides optional authentication. Figure 1.3 depicts an IP packet transformed by ESP in transport mode. The ESP header is located after the IP header. It contains the security parameter index to identify the security association. Furthermore, there is a sequence number that increases by one for each consecutive packet. This helps to detect replay attacks, where the attacker records a packet and re-sends it later. After the payload the ESP trailer is added. The trailer includes a padding. The padding is necessary because the encryption algorithms often require that the payload comes in blocks of a fixed length (e.g. 8 bytes). The pad length field encodes the length of the padding in bits. The next header field contains the protocol number of the next (possibly higher layer) protocol in the payload (e.g. IP or a concatenated IPSec protocol). Note that the trailer up to here is also encrypted. So, an attacker cannot, for example, read what protocol is in the payload data. The ESP trailer may end with optional authentication data. The data is a message authentication code (MAC) computed by a secure hash function. The input of the hash is a secret key, the ESP header, the ESP payload, and the rest of the ESP trailer. The MAC does not protect the initial IP header.

The Authentication Header

The IANA has assigned the protocol number 51 for the IPSec authentication header. AH authenticates the packet so that a receiving IPSec peer can know for sure that the packet originates from the sending peer. Furthermore, the packet integrity is guaranteed. The receiver can verify that nobody has changed the packet while it was in transit between the peers. AH ensures this by calculating authentication data with a secure one-way hash function. The calculation also includes the secret key. An attacker that does not know this key is neither able to forge a valid packet nor to authenticate the packet. Figure 1.4 depicts an IP packet transformed by AH in transport mode. The AH header includes the next header field and encodes the payload length. The length is necessary because the authentication data is variable in length. The AH header, just like the ESP header, contains a security parameter index and a sequence number. Finally, there is the authentication data

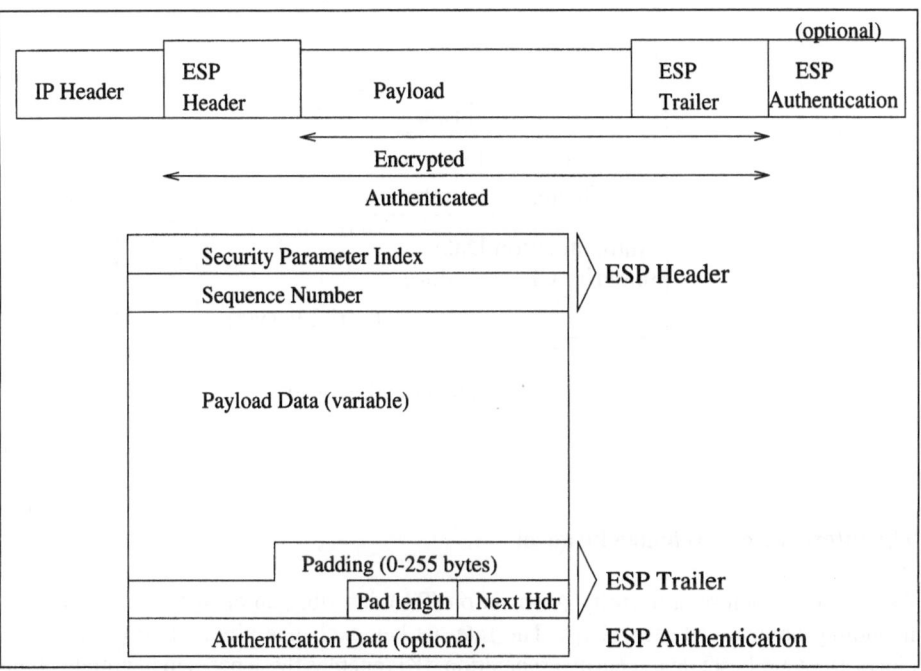

Figure 1.3: The encapsulation security payload.

(the secure hash value). In contrast to the optional authentication of ESP the authentication of AH also covers the original IP header. However, some fields of the IP header are
excluded from the authentication, because their values may change during the forwarding of the packet. These exceptions are the time-to-live field that is decremented by each
router and the Differentiated Services Code Point (DSCP) (see section 1.2.3).

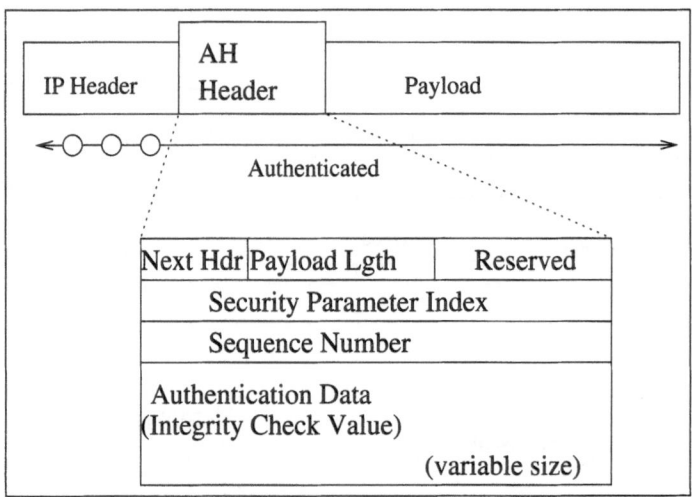

Figure 1.4: The authentication header.

The Internet Key Exchange Protocol

As mentioned before, a Security Association (SA) describes an open IPSec connection,
including the involved secret keys. The Internet key exchange protocol allows two machines to securely set up a security association. IKE enables these peers to negotiate about
the protocol (AH or ESP), the protocol mode, and the cryptographic algorithms to be used.
Furthermore, IKE allows the peers to renew an established security association.

IKE uses the Internet Security Association and Key Management Protocol
(ISAKMP) [MSST98] to exchange messages. ISAKMP provides a framework for authentication and key exchange but does not define a particular key exchange scheme. IKE
uses parts of the key exchange schemes Oakley [Orm98] and SKEME [Kra96].

IKE operates in two phases. In phase 1 the two peers establish a secure authenticated
communication channel (also called ISAKMP security association). In phase 2 security
associations can be established on behalf of other services (most prominently IPSec security associations). Phase 2 exchanges require an existing ISAKMP SA. Several phase
2 exchanges can be protected by one ISAKMP SA and a phase 2 exchange can negotiate
several SAs on behalf of other services.

ISAKMP SAs are bidirectional. The following attributes are used by IKE and are negotiated as part of the ISAKMP SA: encryption algorithm, hash algorithm, authentication method, and initial parameters for the Diffie-Hellman algorithm [Sch96].

Phase 1 Exchange. IKE defines two modes for phase 1 exchanges: main mode and aggressive mode. The main mode consists of three request-response message pairs. The first two messages negotiate policy (e.g. authentication method), the next two messages exchange Diffie-Hellman public values and ancillary data necessary for the key exchange. The last two messages authenticate the Diffie-Hellman exchange. The last two messages are encrypted and conceal the identity of the two peers.

The aggressive mode of phase 1 consists of only three messages. The first message and its reply negotiate policy, exchange Diffie-Hellman public values, ancillary data necessary for the key exchange, and identities. In addition the second message authenticates the responder. The third message authenticates the initiator and provides a proof of participation in the exchange. The final message may be encrypted. Aggressive mode securely exchanges authenticated key material and sets up an ISAKMP SA, but it reveals the identities of the ISAKMP SA peers to eavesdroppers.

Note that the choice of the authentication method influences the specific composition of the payload of this exchange. Keep also in mind that IKE assumes security policies that describe what options can be offered during the IKE negotiation.

Phase 2 Exchange. A phase 2 exchange negotiates security associations for other services and is protected (encrypted and authenticated) based on an existing ISAKMP security association. The payloads of all phase 2 messages are encrypted. A phase 2 exchange consists of three messages. The initiator sends a message containing a hash value, the proposed security association parameters, and a nonce. The hash value is calculated over ISAKMP SA key material and proves authenticity. The nonce prevents replay attacks. Optionally, the initial message can also contain key exchange material. Such an optional phase 2 key exchange generates key material which is independent of the key material of the ISAKMP SA. If the new SA should be broken, the ISAKMP SA is thus not compromised. The initial message may also contain identifiers in case the new SA is to be established between different peers rather than the ISAKMP SA peers.

The responder replies with a message of the same structure as the initial message: an authenticating hash value, the selected SA parameters, and a nonce. If the initial message contained optional parameters, then these would also be part of the reply. Finally, the initiator acknowledges the exchange with a third and final message containing yet another hash value.

Authentication. IKE establishes authenticated keying material. IKE supports four authentication methods to be used in phase 1: pre-shared secret keys, two forms of authentication with public key encryption, and digital signatures. Today's IKE implementations support X.509 certificates. So, two machines that do not know each other can initialize a security association with the help of the commonly trusted third party that verified the certificates.

1.2.3   Differentiated Services (DiffServ)

The best-effort nature of IP forwarding hinders, for example, the deployment of real-time applications. The most recent approach to bring Quality-of-Service (QoS) features, such as small traffic latency or jitter, guaranteed bandwidth, and low loss rates to the Internet, is called Differentiated Services (DiffServ).

Differentiated Services [BBC$^+$98] is a scalable technique that provides QoS in IP networks by traffic aggregation based on Differentiated Services Code Points (DSCP) [NBBB98]. The DSCP is a one-byte field in the IP header. The routers use the DSCP to map each packet to a per-hop behavior. Inside of a DiffServ network, all IP traffic using the same code point is called a DiffServ behavior aggregate and is treated equally. The treatment is defined locally and is called a Per-Hop Behavior (PHB). Since there are only a handful of PHBs, the DiffServ architecture scales also to large core networks.

The IP packets are classified and processed by traffic conditioners at the edge of a DiffServ domain. Thus, most DiffServ related processing is done at the edges of the domains. DiffServ domains are typically equivalent to administrative domains, i.e. a customer premises network or the network of an Internet Service Provider (ISP). A DiffServ service is specified in so-called Service Level Specifications (SLSs). These SLS must be established among the various DiffServ domains. Theses SLSs form the basis for traffic conditioning actions, such as shaping, policing, and remarking at the edge routers.

In order to provide QoS guarantees similar to what customers have been used from leased line services, the Expedited Forwarding (EF) per-hop behavior is the appropriate choice [JNP99]. The EF PHB can be used to build a low latency assured bandwidth end-to-end service through DiffServ domains. Such a service appears to the endpoints like a point-to-point connection or a virtual leased line. A typical SLS for such a service might include the ingress and egress point of the DiffServ domain that will provide the service and a peak rate which can be guaranteed to the traffic stream.

The Assured Forwarding (AF) PHB group [HBWW99] provides different levels of forwarding assurances for IP packets. Four AF classes are defined with three drop precedences each. A typical SLS includes rates for low and medium drop priority packets and might also specify ingress and egress points. AF configuration is considered complex, but it allows the provider to compose a more elaborate and fine-tuned quality-of-service support.

Management of a DiffServ domain can be done using so-called Bandwidth Brokers (BB) [NJZ99, TWOZ99]. Bandwidth brokers are software agents (see section 1.3) that manage DiffServ allocations on behalf of the provider organization. The bandwidth brokers can be configured with organizational policies, keep track of the current allocation of marked traffic, and interpret new requests to mark traffic in light of the policies and current allocation. Inter-domain DiffServ traffic is regulated by the bandwidth brokers according to bilateral SLAs.

1.3 Agent Technology

Software agent technology is an ongoing research issue in several fields of computer science. The term *agent* is 'occupied' by several research communities. Researchers of the artificial intelligence community originally initiated work on so-called *intelligent agents* [MJ99] in order to study computational models of distributed intelligence. Later, the software engineering community (see e.g. [WJ99]) launched a new wave of interest in software agents which should help to simplify the complexities of distributed computing and which could overcome the limitations of current user interface approaches [Bra97].

A software agent is a computer program acting autonomously on behalf of a person or organization. Software agents usually have one or several of the properties [Mil00] of the following list. Note that different agent research communities focus on different sets of these properties. Software agents are:

- **Autonomous.** The agents are proactive; they work towards a goal. The intelligent agent research focuses on how artificial intelligence (inference systems, theorem provers) can enable the agent to autonomously find a solution to a given problem.

- **Adaptive and Reactive.** Agents can react and adapt their behavior to the current state of their environment. Thus, they are 'aware' of their current environment. This property renders agent-based solutions interesting for applications in heterogeneous environments, such as the Internet. Agents may also have the ability to learn and to adapt to uncertainty and to change. This makes agent technology suitable for the interaction with the real world.

- **Mobile.** The autonomy of the agent may also express itself as agent mobility. Such an agent is able to roam in a self-directed way from one execution environment to another execution environment. So-called *mobile agents* [Kna96] are usually smaller and less adaptive than intelligent agents.

- **Communicative and cooperative.** One strength of the agent paradigm lies in the rich functionality that may emerge when many (small) systems interact based on (even simple) rules. All agent systems provide facilities permitting agents to communicate (possibly across computer networks). Some researchers consider communication and cooperation aspects as being so important to the agent paradigm that they simply *define* a software agent as an entity able to communicate in an Agent Communication Language (ACL). Research on ACLs has produced high level languages that do not only communicate sentences, but rather communicate an attitude about the content (e.g. belief, assertion, query etc.). These languages are inspired by the speech act theory of linguistics. A recent language example which gains importance in the said research community is the Foundation for Intelligent Physical Agents (FIPA) ACL [http://www.fipa.org].

- **Interactive.** Agents can inter-operate with other agents, with legacy systems, other information sources, and with humans. The agent paradigm is also used as a metaphor to facilitate the human-to-computer interaction.

- **Delegation.** A human should be able to delegate some of his/her tasks to the agent which will filter, extract, and present the relevant information from bodies of information larger than the human could ordinarily digest. Often, the metaphor of a 'digital butler' is used in this context.

Since the agent paradigm is applied by several research communities, there is no consensus on a specific agent definition. Yet, there is a rough consensus that the presented properties are relevant. Properties that are relevant to all agent systems are the goal-driven autonomy, the environment awareness and the collaboration/communication. Intelligent agents and mobile agents represent specialized instances of the software agent paradigm.

1.4   Network and Service Management

In order to be able to offer new IP services such as DiffServ or VPNs, the providers must deploy a management system that has to set up the device configurations necessary, manage the available network resources and monitor the ongoing services. The telecommunication industry, which is the largest player in the IP network provisioning business, has standardized the Telecommunications Management Network (TMN) model [IT]. The model provides a way to think logically about how the business of a service provider is managed. The model consists of five layers where each layer provides capabilities to its upper neighbor and each layer imposes requirements on its lower neighbor. The components of the lower layers are more distributed and technically oriented. The higher the layer, the more information is concentrated into high-level abstractions. The higher layers can therefore be more centralized, which allows the management system to maintain consistency in the operations. The TMN model is thus usually depicted as a pyramid (see figure 1.5). The business layer contains processes that deal with the corporate strategy and customer relations of the provider. The service layer deals with the products that are offered to the customers, namely the services. The network management layer incorporates the management processes necessary for the provider's overall network infrastructure. The element management concentrates on processes concerning single devices in the network (servers, routers, switches etc.). Finally, there is an element layer representing the heterogeneous hardware devices that form a network.

The processes at all layers go through a more or less similar life cycle (see figure 1.6). After planning (e.g. what equipment to buy, or what service to offer) and deployment, there is a third phase consisting of operation, maintenance, and monitoring. This phase is supposed to generate revenues for the provider. At the end of the cycle an evolution/upgrade phase takes place which may lead to a new planning phase or to withdrawal. The operation phase is ideally the longest phase and is not directly related to strategic decisions. It includes many repetitive tasks (monitoring, accounting, etc.). For these reasons it is feasible and most worthwhile to automate the operation phase.

This book focuses on the service level of the TMN model and particularly on the monitoring task of the operations phase of the service life cycle.

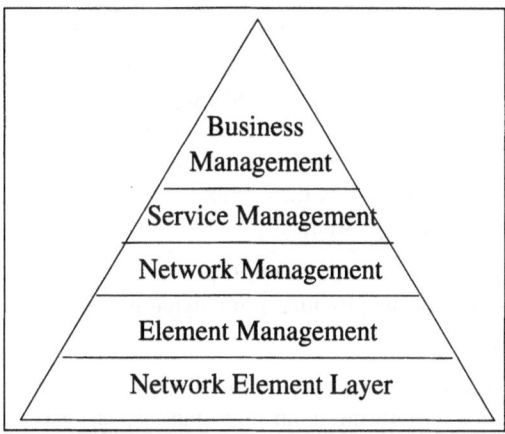

Figure 1.5: Telecommunication management network model.

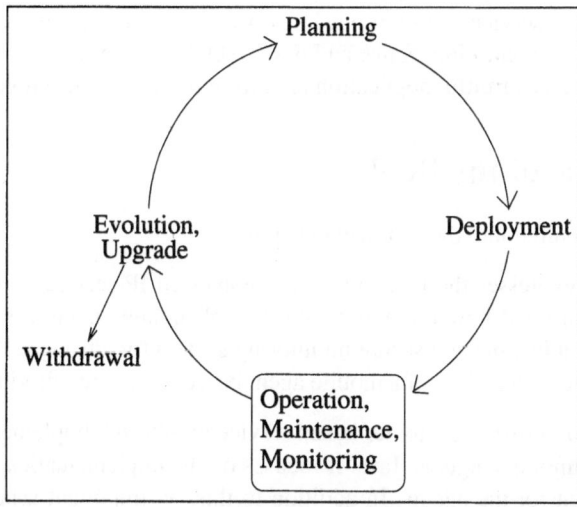

Figure 1.6: Life cycle of management processes.

1.5   The Problem and the Proposed Approach

The TMN is just a reference model. Implementation efforts have been started, however, they usually start bottom-up. There is no standardized service management yet that would allow the provider to offer network services on demand, in other words, automate the service operation phase. We believe that such a management platform will emerge because only then can the providers maximize the revenues of their network infrastructure and survive in a competitive market [GBK99, BGK01]. Note that we studied approaches towards such service management platforms in the original PhD thesis [Gün01].

This book focuses on the question:

> How can the correct operation of a multi-provider IP service be verified (by either the customers or the providers) in a dynamic, convincing, secure, and scalable way?

We present a customer-based service monitoring infrastructure based on mobile software agents. Service monitoring is an important aspect of service management because the monitoring data provides the management system with feedback on the network and service status [GB00].

Both customers and collaborating providers can use the monitoring infrastructure to test the smooth operation of the service and gather traces and evidence of problems. The proposed infrastructure allows the user to delegate monitoring tasks to mobile agents. The agents are programmable, and for this reason they can monitor any kind of emerging IP services. The mobility of the agents can be exploited to efficiently preprocess the monitoring data close to the data source. Furthermore, mobile agent technology eases the deployment of new service testing procedures. Based on an implementation and practical examples (VPN monitoring, active and passive QoS monitoring) this book shows that service monitoring is a fruitful application area for mobile agent technology.

1.6   Outline of the Book

This book is structured into the following chapters:

- Chapter 2 expresses the motivation why enhanced IP services need a monitoring infrastructure and how the unique abilities of mobile agents can be exploited to implement a flexible and secure monitoring system for advanced IP services. It introduces the architecture of a mobile agent based service monitoring infrastructure.

- Chapter 3 describes a customer-based service monitoring implementation based on the programming language Java. It focuses on the implementation of the execution environment for the agents. In addition to this, an important aspect is the implementation of security and resource control mechanisms.

- Chapter 4 demonstrates the implementation of mobile agents that monitor a number of advanced IP services, such as a virtual private network service and Differentiated Services. The chapter also presents future applications.

- Chapter 5 presents performance statistics of the implemented monitoring infrastructure. It shows that the performance is sufficient to enable interesting monitoring applications.

- Chapter 6 discusses related research efforts in the area of monitoring of advanced IP services. This chapter compares the related work to the approach proposed in this book.

- Chapter 7 concludes the book.

Chapter 2

A Service Monitoring Architecture

2.1 Introduction and Motivation

Traditional network management includes monitoring of the network. The monitoring serves several purposes: it verifies the smooth operation of the network, it alarms the administration in case of an anomaly and it provides usage and performance data for future network provisioning and planning [CC98]. The customers of an Internet service provider are neither directly interested in monitoring the network of the provider nor should they be allowed to do so. However, the customers may want to monitor their enhanced IP service. The enhancement of the service is normally transparent to the customer, because it consists of differentiated packet processing that happens in the provider networks. The providers offer enhanced services to generate new revenues. Therefore, enhanced services will cost more than basic IP services. Since the customer pays for the service enhancement, the customer has a vital interest to possess an explicit means to verify the enhancement and thus justify the additional expenses.

The monitoring needs vary from customer to customer and from service to service. In order to convince the customer of the usefulness and stability of a new service, the provider must offer a generic service monitoring interface. The interface should allow the customer to verify the correct operation of the service functionalities sold by the provider. We refer to this process as Customer-based Service Monitoring (CSM). The provisioning of such a monitoring interface may be crucial for the successful introduction of new commercial Internet services because only that way the customer sees what (s)he buys. Consider the virtual private network service described in chapter 1.2.1. How can a customer know that the traffic traveling through the Internet is indeed encrypted by the provider and, for instance, not just compressed? How can the customer see if regular Internet traffic backs off when the customer sends prioritized DiffServ traffic? How can the customer find out that prioritized traffic has been dropped in the network (and not e.g.

by an application) and where (by whom) it was dropped? How can the customer verify that a specific service level agreement with the provider is indeed fulfilled?

A generic Internet service monitoring infrastructure provided by the ISPs to their customers can answer such questions. It provides a means for the service providers to convince customers of the usefulness of new Internet services. The provider can also describe the service level guarantees in terms of the monitoring infrastructure. The more powerful the monitoring interface is, the more sophisticated service level agreements can be formulated. Thus, a generic CSM infrastructure allows the provider to differentiate their service offerings. There are, however, many problems that make customer-based service monitoring significantly more complex than simple network monitoring:

- **Service-specific monitoring.** New Internet services provide different add-on features to traditional IP forwarding. These features can have all kinds of service specific parameters. The monitoring infrastructure must be generic enough to support different metrics for service-specific traffic parameters.

- **Individual customer wishes.** The customers may order a service based on different requirements resulting from different business backgrounds. It should be possible for each customer to test the service against his/her individual requirements using customer defined metrics. The customer should also be able to test the service at any time.

- **Multiple providers.** In case several providers collaborate to provide an end-to-end service, the monitoring should provide per-provider information. This is desirable especially when providers are customers of each other and to detect ill-intended/cheating providers.

- **Security.** Network monitoring data is sensitive, revealing it to others violates the customers' and the providers' privacy. The data may reveal organizational details that competitors can use against a provider. Also, a provider will lose its customers if they ever find out that other parties may monitor customer service traffic. Thus, the service monitoring infrastructure must be protected against ill-intended customers. Furthermore, the integrity of the monitoring data must be protected. It is desirable that the monitoring infrastructure discourages ill-intended providers.

- **Standardization.** Although the parameters to be monitored may vary greatly, the monitoring infrastructure should be standardized. This eases the deployment in a multi-provider scenario and allows rapid development of application software by third-parties.

Today, no service monitoring infrastructure exists that meets these requirements. If a customer happens to detect a problem (which is usually when the customer needs that service badly and does not get it), phone-calls between administrators, local measurements, and manual browsing of log-files will eventually lead to the identification of the problem source. Unfortunately, often the involved parties will suspect each other and repudiate any guilt. Note that this problem does not only concern the relation between customer and provider but also between providers themselves. It is to be expected that the problem becomes worse when new and more expensive network services are deployed that require provider collaboration. First steps towards a service monitoring infrastructure are SLA reports [Ver99]. The provider calculates a performance statistics over a regular period of time (e.g. once a month). The statistics usually reflects the traffic properties guaranteed in the SLA (e.g. uptime and response time). The provider then delivers this statistics to its customer on a regular basis (usually once a month). Nevertheless, this approach does not satisfy the requirements of a generic service monitoring infrastructure. The customer is not able to formulate individual queries whenever (s)he feels like it. The provider can very easily manipulate the statistics to meet a given SLA. The statistics, the collection of their raw data and their delivery to the customer are not standardized and the customer cannot tailor them to individual wishes.

This book introduces a generic service monitoring infrastructure based on mobile agents. Mobile agents provide a flexible way to monitor the services *within* provider networks (for further motivation see section 2.2). The customer thus sends mobile test agents to relevant locations in the provider networks. The agents perform tests on behalf of the customer. In this way mobile agents allow the customer to test the service where it is delivered. A customer-based service monitoring infrastructure based on mobile agents can solve the problems mentioned above. With agent technology service performance is no longer formulated as statistics of some network parameters. Agents are programmable and can thus measure any metrics on the raw data. Therefore, agent technology provides a generic interface that the customers, providers or third-party vendors can easily adapt to new services or individual customer wishes. The mobility of the agents reduces communication overhead and supports the distribution of monitoring tasks, which increases the scalability of the approach. The mobility of the agents also helps to detect misbehavior of providers since the customer can collect distributed measurements and compare their global consistency. Agent security is a well-known research area where complete solutions exist today. Standardization and internationalization can be achieved through the use of state-of-the-art technology, such as the Java programming language.

2.2 Mobility and Service Monitoring

2.2.1 Terminology

Mobile agents [Whi94, CHK97] are program instances that are able to move in a self-directed way through a network to locally perform a task on behalf of their sender. Different mobile agent platforms have been proposed, e.g. for the programming languages Java [LO98, VB99, Fün98] and Tcl [Gra98]. Mobile agents are introduced for different tasks, such as e-commerce [HGF+99], network management [BGP97], and network intrusion detection [JMKM99].

On the network level, the emerging mobile agents technology is called *active networking* [TSS+97, CBZS98]. There, a mobile agent is often referred to as *capsule* and is directly integrated into the network traffic packets. Thus, the code flows directly on the communication path that is subject to the code's computation and it can be executed on a per-packet granularity. Here, the abstraction and intelligence aspect is secondary. The focus is rather on the interaction with the network infrastructure. Active network packets access the networking functionalities (e.g. forwarding and routing) of the routers through which they pass and change these functionalities for packets or classes of packets. Furthermore, performance is a crucial issue, since the code should be able to manipulate data at the line speed (in today's backbone network this can be up to several gigabits per second). Active networking is often proposed for intelligent multicasting. Another possible application is secure communication [GBB01, Bro00, Tsc00].

There is no solid line between mobile agents and active networking. For example, the active networking testbed ANTS [WGT98] can also be seen as a mobile agent testbed, since capsules are Java objects, and the code is not included in network data packets but is dynamically loaded upon need. The approach that we describe in this paper is mobile agent based. This is because the monitoring code (the mobile agents) is transported out-of-band. Yet, service monitoring agents examine network services down to the structure of forwarded network packets. Equally, the performance of the CSM agents is an issue as one of their goals can be to monitor the network at wire speed. For these reasons, CSM can also be seen as an application of active networking. The implementation of the CSM system which we are going to present is mobile agent based. Nevertheless, similar results could have been achieved when choosing active networking technology instead.

2.2.2 Advantages of Service Monitoring with Mobile Agents

Mobile Agents have the questionable reputation of being a solution in search of a problem (J. Ousterhout). However, there are application areas where the use of mobile agents has undeniable benefits [Kna96]. This section outlines their benefits for service monitoring. The programmability of mobile agents has the following advantages already mentioned in the beginning of this part: flexibility, available security solutions, and standard technology. The mobility of the agents also brings substantial benefits:

- **Working at the monitored site.** Network services are by definition delivered *in* the provider network. In the case of multi-provider services the service enabling functions even take place in several networks. On the other hand it is mainly the customer who wants to perform the service tests and not the administrator of the networks in question. Given the already mentioned advantages of being able to formulate service tests as programs, the solution obviously is that the customer *sends* the test program to the interesting locations in the network. Given security and multi-user requirements, the proper way to do so from the software engineering point of view is to send mobile agents.

- **Performance.** Generic measurements, such as packet traces, produce a huge amount of raw data which is of the same order of magnitude as the traffic being monitored. Therefore, traditional customer-based monitoring infrastructures always calculate statistics over the raw data for a medium to long period of time.

Thus, the raw data is compressed before delivered to the customer. Mobile agents can do this compression in a flexible way, thus keeping the communication path short. This can also reduce latency of the detection of a service anomaly. Furthermore, the mobile agents can implement the extraction of relevant data in optimized ways. Thus, they may execute faster than general purpose filters. If one compression step does not reduce the communication sufficiently, the mobility of the agents can be exploited to build a communication hierarchy. In general, mobile agents are a powerful method to structure distributed computing thereby enabling the customer to collect computing power in order to analyze the traffic.

- **Global view of the service.** An ill-intended provider can easily fool a customer who relies on the measurements published by the provider. In a multi-provider service scenario the situation is even worse. CSM agents can be sent out to perform active measurements by producing and measuring traffic at different sites that are out of the administrative domain of the provider to be tested. The agents can thus provide different views of the current service state, which an ill-intended provider cannot directly influence. In general, a provider who tries to fake a service state cannot keep the views consistent. Mobility therefore allows the agents to virtually 'track-down' the problem source (see section 4.4).

- **Independence.** In case of a service interruption (e.g. a complete network failure) at least some CSM agents will still be running and can continue to record the service performance. Later, that information may help to find the source of the problem or to negotiate about refunding.

2.3 The Basic Infrastructure for Service Monitoring Agents

Like any other network monitoring system, the CSM agents need a supporting infrastructure. In this section we discuss the required components and their location in the providers' networks.

2.3.1 Location of the Control Points

The Internet is a heterogeneous network, it consists of thousands of administrative domains. The interior network of these domains is administered in different ways and is composed of different kinds of networking technologies, such as Frame Relay, ATM, MPLS or Sonet. This may render access to the traffic inside of the domain very difficult (e.g. for optically switched technology). The least common denominator of these networks is the Internet Protocol (IP). The IP traffic is exchanged between the domains at so-called peering points, according to peering or service level agreements. While the network engineering and management of the interior network of the domains is usually hidden, the peering points are by their nature open (at least to the peer). For service monitoring the peering points are thus of high interest. Note that for CSM it suffices to track down a problem to a provider. Once the problem is found relating to a given administrative domain, it is up to its administration to further locate the problem in the inside of their network, using the network management system of their choice. Therefore, the CSM agent nodes should be located at the peering points. This guarantees that the monitoring has access to the IP traffic and that the control can relate identified problems to a specific provider. Note that not all CSM applications will need a platform at all peering points. Of course, a provider can also offer additional node environments in the inside of its network as an additional service to its customers or for its own service and network monitoring purposes.

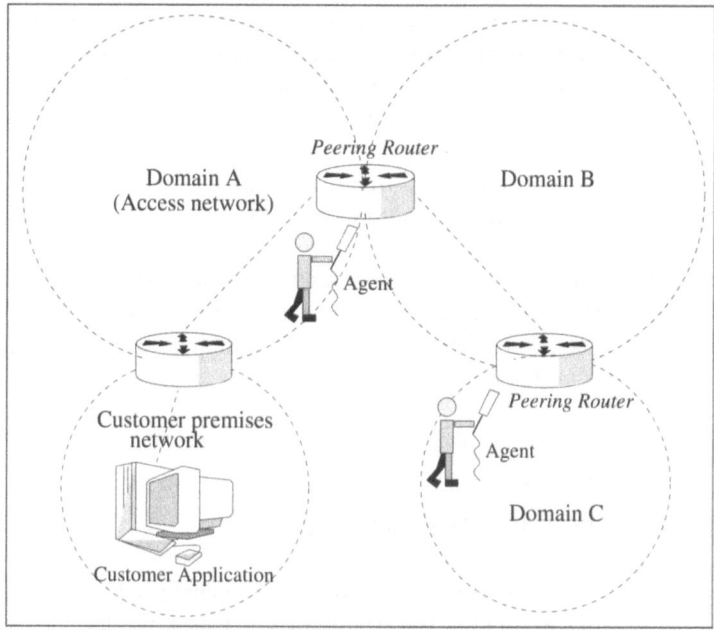

Figure 2.1: Measuring at peering points.

Figure 2.1 illustrates CSM agents which were sent out by a customer application running on a machine owned by the customer. The customer application also coordinates the agents, processes their feedback and forwards the results to the user. The agents migrate to the peering points to perform particular local checks on the service.

2.3.2   Node Architecture

The CSM agents should be able to perform any kind of passive measurements, however, they should not be able to eavesdrop or analyze traffic of other customers. Spoofing of foreign IP addresses or denial-of-service attacks should not be facilitated. Given these requirements we propose the following node architecture as depicted in figure 2.2: at the peering router, there is a *T-component* that serves as a high-performance and configurable packet copying mechanism. The T-component can be configured to copy network packets according to filtering rules based on IP packet information, such as source and destination address (see section 2.3.3). It adds a high-accuracy time-stamp to the packet. Note that this is in fact the *generic Internet service monitoring interface*. By being able to examine all relevant IP packets and their arrival times, each IP service and its service level can be analyzed. The T-component forwards the requested packet copies to the *Node environment*. Keep in mind that for security reasons the agents do *not* have direct access to the T-component.

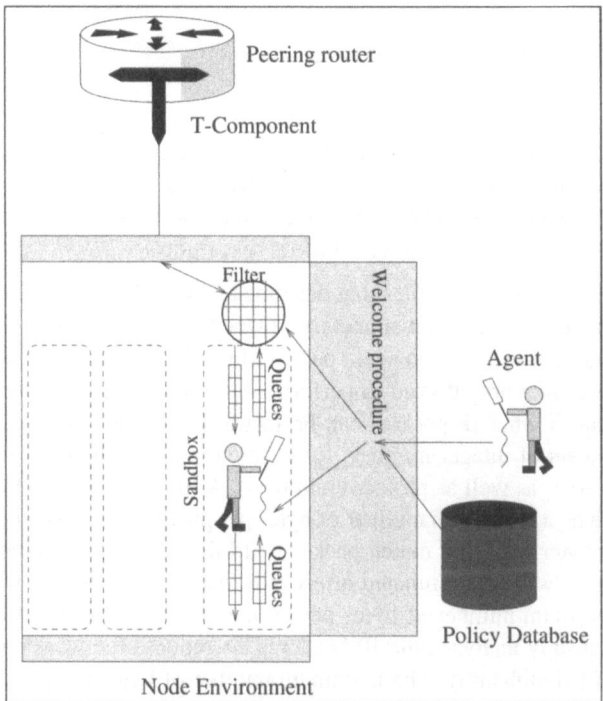

Figure 2.2: The node environment.

The *node environment* hosts and executes the CSM agents. Separating the node environment and the T-component enables the provider to run the node environment on a separate machine (with network connection to the T-component). Most providers probably will not want to run foreign code on such a crucial machine as the peering router. Customers send their agents to the node using a standardized protocol (see section 3.1). The agent does not necessarily have to be encrypted, but a strong authentication protocol is needed. This ensures that the node can properly authorize the agent. When the agent arrives at a node, it has to undergo a welcome procedure. After the authentication, the agent asks the node for resources (CPU time, memory, and specific traffic). The agent also specifies a packet filter for the bypassing packets in which it is interested (see section 2.3.3). Based on policies, the node authorizes the agent for these resources. It provides an execution environment that protects the node from the agent and agents from other agents. The agent execution environment also contains an inbound and an outbound packet queue. The inbound queue provides the agent with the monitored IP packets. The outbound queue permits the agent to communicate across the Internet. Using another pair of queues, the agent can order services from the node and receive the results of these services (e.g. information about neighbor nodes - see section 3.3.4).

2.3.3   Authorization and Filtering

Each agent is associated with a customer of Internet services and has to authenticate itself as an agent of that customer. The customer digitally signs the agent to guarantee its authenticity. Note that in some cases customers may want the possibility to send anonymous agents. These agents should not be signed in order not to reveal the identity of the customer. Anonymous agents must have little access rights.

The node has access to profiles that describe among other things the administrative domain of the customer (e.g. what subnets are owned by that customer - see also section 3.3.5). The profiles also refer to an agent policy which describes what kind of actions the agents of that customer are allowed to perform. An important part of that description is the *filter*. It explains what IP packets can be forwarded to the agents of that customer. The filter holds a set of integer numbers for different parts of the IP header (source and destination addresses as well as protocol numbers). A filter can also contain a maximum number of matches, a maximum number of bytes per packet to be copied, and a matching probability. The filter will only match packets until the maximum number of matches is reached. The agent will be terminated afterwards. The maximum number can be set to infinity. The maximum number of bytes per packet can be used, for instance, to formulate an agent that only analyzes the IP header. This reduces the workload of both node and T-component significantly. The maximum number of bytes per packet can be set to any (2^{16} bytes). The matching probability is usually set to 1.0. The matching probability is useful to support an Embedded Advanced Sampling Environment (EASE) [CC98] architecture where only a certain percentage (usually 2%) of the traffic is analyzed. At the same time, the matching probability provides a means to reduce the workload of the CSM infrastructure, especially in backbone environments.

The node will only feed the agent with those IP packets that match the filter. The agent also carries a filter with it to tell the node what kind of IP packets it is interested in. The node calculates the mathematical cut between the policy filter and the agents filter and uses this newly created filter to serve packets to the agent. The new filter forwards all packets that were requested by the agent (that match the agent's filter) and that are also compliant with the filter of the policy. The agent can query if the new filter is empty (matches no packets at all) or not equal to what it has requested, and react upon this (e.g. terminate gracefully). The node holds filter templates in its policies so that it does not need to keep a filter for each potential customer. See section 3.3.5 for implementation details.

2.3.4 Security Issues

The security of the proposed infrastructure bases on three concepts. First and foremost, the agents must authenticate themselves with strong cryptography. Developing these mechanisms from scratch is tedious and probably insecure. For this reason CSM rather relies on existing and stable technology, such as PGP [Zim01], or built-in mechanisms of available agent platforms. Authentication allows the node to relate each agent to a customer, which is responsible for the behavior of the agent. Second, the agents do not run on the controlled network devices but rather on a dedicated general-purpose computer. Thirdly, the agents run in a sand-box. They have no direct access to either node or network resources. Their only communication mechanism uses the in- and outbound queues which are controlled by node filters. The cutting of agent filters with a default filter provided by the node assures in a convenient way that the agents cannot eavesdrop or spoof other people's traffic. The implementation of these security features is described in more detail in section 3.5.

2.4 Mobility Models and Agent Forwarding

CSM uses a simple mobility model that is inspired more by the active networking community than by the mobile agent community. One reason is that the envisioned applications for mobile measurement agents can be implemented by agents that are sent to a location, perform their measurement there while sending some results and then terminate. For such an application it is simply not necessary that the agent can roam in a self-directed way through the networks [BLP00]. Self-directed agents need well-founded knowledge about the network and a more complex communication infrastructure. However, measurement agents should be small and simple so that customers can program them. This favors a simple send-execute-terminate style of mobility. Nevertheless, sending out many agents one-by-one is a tedious and inefficient procedure. Therefore, we propose mobility support that is simple, secure and efficient.

2.4.1 Supported Mobility Models

As mentioned above, the proposed mobility model is inspired by active networking. There, executable data packets (capsules) are forwarded through the network and get executed wherever there is an execution environment. Ideally, they are executed in every router. This is convenient because then the capsules do not need sophisticated knowledge about the network. They can rely on the local routing information. For CSM, however, there is no built-in support that extracts the agents from the data stream. CSM is a non-intrusive Internet application that does not assume CSM specific execution environments in the routers. Instead, the CSM nodes provide *agent forwarding* functionality: an agent that arrives at a node is copied, just like a data packet would have been, and the copy is forwarded to other nodes, if requested.

We propose different kinds of forwarding modes as follows:

- **No forwarding.** An agent arriving in this trivial mode is executed at the node but not forwarded to any other node. This model is also referred to as sending an agent *end-to-end*.

- **Broadcast.** A broadcasted agent is first started in the target node. If the agent starts without causing problems (e.g. false authentication), the agent is forwarded (in broadcast mode) to all neighbor nodes. Agents have an identity which is defined by a serial number and the owner's identifier. Each execution environment executes only one agent of a given identity. Thus, the broadcast terminates similarly to a flooding algorithm.

- **Hop-by-hop.** The agent carries a destination IP or node address. The node starts the agent. If the agent starts without causing problems, the node forwards it (in hop-by-hop mode) to the next node on the route towards the destination address. For that purpose the nodes need access to routing information (see section 3.7.2).

The broadcast mode allows the customer to easily and efficiently spread agents, e.g. to monitor a service at as many locations as possible. The hop-by-hop mode is useful to watch the service behavior along a path, e.g. between two customer subnets connected through the Internet with a VPN tunnel (see chapter 4). It is obvious that both broadcasting and hop-by-hop forwarding save communication capacity when a user wants to install an agent at many nodes. Of course the forwarding of the agents must be limited. Therefore, the agent transmission protocol should carry a time-to-live field that is decremented for each agent instance being executed. Another interesting feature is the use of forwarding probabilities. For example, broadcasting an agent with a small forwarding probability could be used to cover a local area with the agent. Another interesting scheme is the hop-by-hop scheme combined with a probability regulated broadcast to cover an area around a network path. The probability idea could be extended with the introduction of an execution probability. The forwarding would then be decoupled from the execution. Some nodes would, for example, just forward an agent but not execute it. This allows sparse distribution of agents. Yet, when only agents that execute without a problem are forwarded, this increases security and reduces the possibility of a denial-of-service attack. Note that a possible model extension is described in section 4.5.2.

2.4.2 Forwarding Security

Since the forwarding of agents allows a customer to request resources at many places at (almost) the same time, all agents that request forwarding (and thus multiplying) must be strongly authenticated. The customer signs the agent before sending it. Note that this scheme rules out strong mobility for the agent. To support strong mobility, the node has to send the run-time state of the agent. The state changes when the agent is roaming in the network, and so the signature is invalidated. The solution would be that the executing node digitally signs the agent. But how can the node take responsibility for the agent in the new state? Think of an agent that develops ill-intentioned behavior if it gets in a certain state. The customer signs the static code while the node signs the state. Who is to blame for the ill-intended behavior? Maybe a previous node manipulated the state so that the agent became unsafe or maybe the customer planned the whole attack. In the CSM approach the customer is fully responsible and (s)he signs the whole agent code. The node only forwards copies of that code. The customer's signature stays valid. However, the node first executes the agent and thus, when it forwards the agent, it guarantees that the agent is executable. The node can also additionally sign the forwarded agent to increase security. As mentioned before, the forwarding must be limited to a finite number of executions by a time-to-live field value which may be authenticated by the nodes. It cannot be authenticated by the customer because the hosting nodes decrement the number in the field.

2.5 Deployment of the CSM Infrastructure in the Internet

The CSM architecture is non-intrusive. It can be deployed step-by-step. There is no need to change the network topology or the protocol stacks. The CSM infrastructure can be deployed based on off-the-shelf technology (see chapter 3). The CSM node can, for example, run in any Java enabled device; it does not require specialized hardware. The architecture can be deployed by a single provider in order to offer an additional service to its customers that offers transparency in the providers service operation and thus builds up trust. Of course, the more providers deploy the CSM infrastructure, the more value it will get.

2.5.1 Advanced Infrastructure Support

If the customer only uses the end-to-end transmission of agents and if the customer only sends agents to a handful of well-known nodes, then no further infrastructure support is needed. However, if there are thousands of nodes and some of their network addresses change from time to time, then the customer will have trouble to distribute its agents to interesting places. One option that the customer has is to use the forwarding modes when sending agents. However, then the providers themselves will face the same problem. Especially for the hop-by-hop mode the node then needs solve a node routing problem.

There are three distinct problems to be addressed:

- **Naming.** CSM nodes and the customers need a name space in which they possess a unique identity. This is also important for signing and encrypting messages. There, the name must identify a public key.

- **Contact information.** Nodes may have different addresses than the routers to be monitored. Nodes may also be moved. Several nodes may be located on a single machine. There must be a way to look up the contact information matching a node name. This may include the IP address, port numbers, and possibly a public key.

- **Routing information.** For agent broadcasting each node must know its neighbor nodes. For hop-by-hop forwarding each node must have access to the IP routing and must also know the topology of the nodes.

The solution to these problems has to be flexible. It must automatically adapt to changes. The solution should also scale to the large size of the Internet. Nevertheless, these problems are not new. Other IP technologies, such as electronic mail, have faced the naming and contact information problem. Also, IP routing was improved to meet the requirements. Therefore, these solutions can also be extended to incorporate support for the CSM infrastructure.

The naming and contact information could rely on the domain name lookup system (DNS) [Moc87a, Moc87b]. Nodes and providers are thus identified by email-style names. The DNS node records are extended to contain a record which includes the contact information. Customers can then use DNS queries that use the available name server hierarchy to learn about the CSM nodes.

For the routing information a node should be able to query the routing table of the router that it monitors. This provides IP routing support. For node routing, the border gateway protocol (BGP-4) [RL95] could be extended. BGP is the state-of-the-art Internet routing protocol for the routing between autonomous systems (provider networks). The node routing also takes place at the inter-domain level. Therefore, it makes sense to add CSM parameters to BGP's optional parameters in order to propagate reachability information of CSM nodes. Note that we did not specify or implement these extensions in more detail. The implementation provides this functionality with an overlay routing system (see section 3.7.2) and is prototypical (see section 3.7).

This presented customer-based service monitoring architecture is the basis for service monitoring with mobile agents. Since the architecture is non-intrusive and only relies on basic agent mechanisms, such as authentication and an execution sand-box which is state of the art, a platform like this can be deployed in the Internet.

Chapter 3

Implementation of a Customer-based Service Monitoring System

This chapter describes an instance of the proposed customer-based service monitoring infrastructure that is implemented in Java [Sunb, Fla96] (version 1.1.8). For several reasons the Java language is suitable for the implementation. First of all Java is a modern and object-oriented language with powerful built-in support for Internetworking (see section 3.1.2). Java is platform independent, supports character internationalization and is a widely-accepted industry standard. Today, most of the modern mobile agent platforms are implemented in Java (see e.g. the mobile agent list [Hoh], [LO98, VB99, Fün98, SBB$^+$00] to mention but a few).

The CSM implementation is divided into three distinct programs that communicate over TCP sockets as depicted in figure 3.1. A *home application* allows the customer to send agents into the network. The program provides a graphical user interface that can also display the measurement and monitoring results sent back by the agents. The application can also store these results on non-volatile media for analysis with other tools. Section 3.6 describes the home application in more detail.

The *CSM node* executes the customers' agents ensuring that no policy is violated. The program is run by the providers. The CSM node is the most complex part of the CSM implementation and is described in section 3.3. It is connected to one or several border routers and aware of the neighbor providers' peer nodes. This is necessary for agent forwarding which was described in section 2.4.

The CSM node obtains the monitored IP packets from the T-component. The node tells the T-component what traffic its agents want to monitor and then receives matching IP packets encapsulated in a TCP connection.

This chapter first describes the CSM protocol (section 3.1) because this protocol provides the interface between the customer (home application) and the provider (CSM

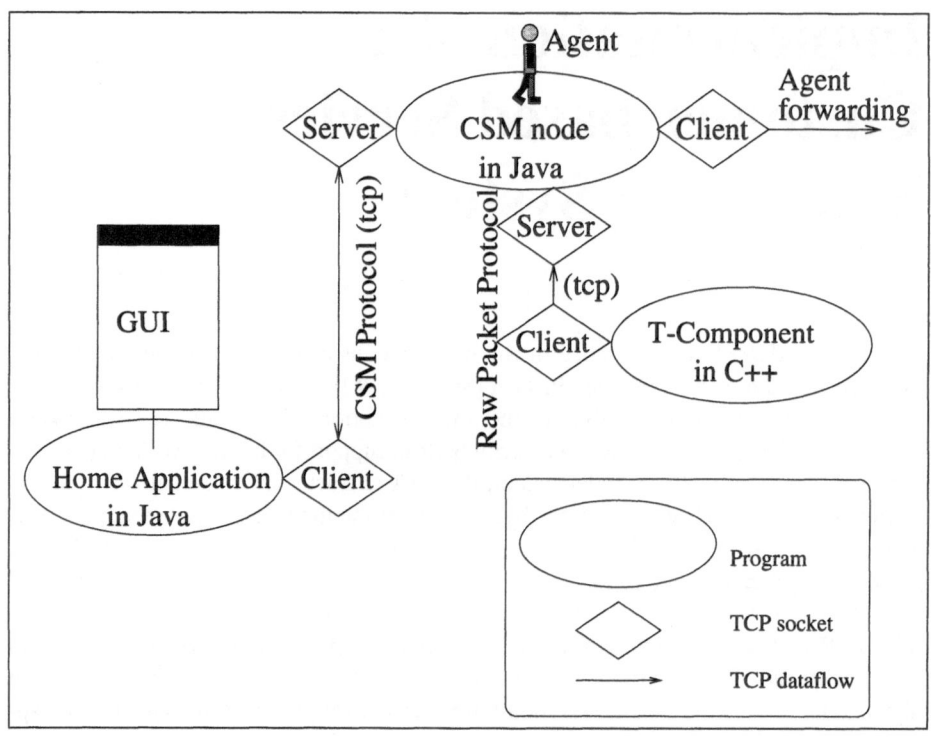

Figure 3.1: Implementation overview.

node). Then section 3.2 defines the T-component and the protocol to transmit the IP packet copies towards the CSM node. After these two protocols will be described, which are important to the CSM node, section 3.3 presents the node implementation. Section 3.4 describes the CSM agent interface that customer agents must implement. Then, section 3.5 discusses the implemented security features of the agents, the node, and the CSM protocol. Section 3.6 explains the implementation of a home application. Section 3.7 presents the implemented Internetworking support (routing, naming) and section 3.8 defines the implementation's source code packaging.

3.1 The CSM Protocol

3.1.1 Overview

The CSM protocol mainly implements the sending of an agent to the CSM node. However, it also provides further means of communication between the home application and the node. The home application can, for example, query the node about the node policies and available resources. Furthermore, the forwarding/multicast of an agent from one node to other nodes is also implemented by the CSM protocol. The CSM protocol is a client-server protocol. The home application (or a forwarding node) acts as a client and contacts the server of a CSM node. Messages are encoded as Java objects. The Java object serialization [Suna] is used to transform the objects into a byte stream that can be transmitted along a TCP connection.

3.1.2 Internet Communication with Java

This section presents useful Java Internetworking features that made Java the first choice for the implementation of an agent platform. It also shows how these features can be combined to create an open, extensible, and generic interface for CSM communication.

Java is the first programming language designed from scratch with networking in mind [Har97]. The necessary classes are bundled in the `java.net` and the `java.io` package. Network programming in Java is simple and intuitive. The client creates a new socket object, opens the socket and writes to the sockets output stream or reads from its input stream. The `accept` method of a server socket returns an open (client) socket that can be used by a separate thread to allow multiple clients to connect to the server concurrently. Java provides built-in primitives for the handling and coordination of concurrent threads [Lea97]. Furthermore, Java includes a uniform concept for exception handling allowing the programmer to catch network exceptions and to react in appropriate ways. With Java the programmer can thus more easily write compact networking code than with other comparable languages, such as C or C++.

Besides of these basic Java features the implementation of the CSM protocol uses two higher level networking concepts of the Java programming language: object serialization and class loaders.

Object serialization. In object-oriented languages [Bud91, BL94], such as Java, the data at run-time is represented as objects. An object holds a reference to its class which in turn defines the methods (operations) that can be called on that object. The class also defines the instance variables that each object holds during its lifetime. The instance variables can be primitive data types, such as integer numbers, or they can hold references to other objects. Thus, at run-time data is usually represented in object hierarchies (objects that recursively refer to other objects via instance variables). Java's object serialization [Suna] provides the programmer a powerful mechanism to transform an object (and recursively all objects referred to by instance variables) into a byte stream. Of course, the serialization mechanism also allows objects of the same class to be instantiated by such a byte stream (deserialization). The bytes of a byte stream can, for example, be stored on disk for later retrieval and deserialization (new instantiation) of an object. The byte stream is also ideal for the transmission of an entire object hierarchy along a network connection.

With few exceptions (such as e.g. `java.io.Stream`) all Java objects and objects of user defined classes can be serialized. All the programmer has to do is to declare his/her new class to be serializable. A user defined class is serializable when it implements the interface `java.io.Serializable`. Doing this is in fact trivial since the declaration does not imply the implementation of new methods. Note that all classes of the instance variables must be declared serializable as well, else a runtime exception will occur.

Java's object serialization renders the tedious task of defining a message data format superfluous. We do not have to fix the format of the messages exchanged in the CSM protocol down to the bits and bytes. Instead, the CSM implementation provides a message class whose objects carry the necessary data in instance variables. The protocol is thus very easily extendible through subclassing of the message class. To wrap up, the serialization mechanism allows us to use objects as flexible and extensible data structures that can be sent over a network connection. Furthermore, Java's object serialization also features basic version control. If the class definition has changed between serialization and deserialization, Java throws an exception.

Class loader. The Java class loader [Mac96] enables the programmer to load new classes at runtime and instantiate objects of these new classes. All the class loader needs to know is an abstract super class or a Java interface of the new object's class. `java.io.Classloader` implements the instantiation functionalities. However, it is an abstract class; the programmer must add a method to fetch the bytecode. The method could, for instance, load the bytecode from disk or download it from a URL. Java capable web browsers, for example, extend the class loader to fetch applets. All their class loader knows in advance is the abstract class `java.applet.Applet`. When an applet is started, the class loader fetches the applet's bytecode from the URL provided in the `html` tag `<applet>`. CSM implements a class loader that obtains the bytecode of CSM agents from message objects sent across a socket. Java's class loader concept allows the

CSM nodes to dynamically load the agents code; thus it provides code mobility. The class loader concept is well integrated into other Java concepts (e.g. security), it is well tested and ubiquitously used in modern web browsers.

3.1.3 Layering of the CSM Protocol

The developers of a CSM application can structure their internal data representation the way they think will fit best. The CSM protocol describes how information is exchanged between a CSM client and a CSM server, including involved data structures. The implementation bundles the CSM protocol in a Java package called `clientserver` (see section 3.8). The package contains classes to transmit CSM information across the Internet. The classes provide a layered protocol stack which is described in table 3.1. Transmission of CSM information is processed top-down and receiving is processed bottom-up.

Table 3.1: CSM communication layers.

Layer	Functionality	Data representation
Semantics	Processes, stores, and generates data in application specific ways.	Application specific objects.
CSM Protocol	Generates and parses the CSM message sequences.	`clientserver.Message` objects
CSM Connection	Opens and closes connections. Encodes (encrypts) message objects and packs them into ProtocolObjects.	`clientserver.Protocol-Object` objects
Network	Byte transmission over TCP.	Serialized `clientserver.Protocol-Object` objects

3.1.4 The Protocol Object

The class `clientserver.ProtocolObject` encapsulates all messages that can be exchanged in the CSM protocol. This simplifies the protocol since only one class of objects is transmitted. The object's class is declared to be serializable so that it can be sent across the network.

```
public class ProtocolObject implements Serializable {
    public String senderID;
    public byte encoding;
    public byte messageType;
    public ForwardingDescriptor forwarding;
    public ByteArray message;
...
}
```

The senderID field holds an identifier of the sender. This instance variable is also used by the node to associate an agent with a customer. The message itself is serialized into the byte array which is hold by the instance variable message. The byte array may hold a message that is signed or encrypted in different ways. The instance variable encoding tells what kind of encoding/encryption scheme is used. The CSM protocol implementation supports PGP encryption, PGP signatures [Zim01], and plain bytecode. Note that PGP encryption also compresses the messages. The instance variable messageType encodes the communication purpose of this object. It signals the type of the object stored in the message instance variable (see also section 3.1.5). The forwarding descriptor is a class of its own that encodes if this message is handled only by the receiver or if it has to be forwarded, and if so, in what way (see section 2.4). The implementation supports two special forwarding modes: broadcasting and hop-by-hop routing. Both forwarding modes are limited by the time-to-live field in the forwarding descriptor, which is decremented for every execution of the agent. As mentioned before, the message instance variable holds the encoded protocol message. To put a message (object of a subclass of clientserver.Message - see next section) into a ByteArray, the message is first serialized. Then, the resulting byte stream may be additionally encoded/encrypted. This is a transformation from one byte stream into another byte stream. The resulting bytes are finally stored in the instance variable of the ProtocolObject. Figure 3.2 shows how messages are encapsulated in the protocol object, which is then transmitted over the network. The CSM protocol can be easily extended by subclassing the message class and adding the newly desired data as well as features to it. In addition to this, new encoding/encryption schemes and forwarding descriptors can be added.

3.1.5   Message Objects

Table 3.2 briefly describes the seven message objects (see also figure 3.2) defined for CSM communication purposes and their message type code.

Supported Queries.   The CSM query is an instrument for the customer to get information about the available CSM support offered by the providers. Basically, the customer sends a query message to a node. The query contains a type code and optional arguments. Like all CSM messages the query is sent within a ProtocolObject. The node can therefore associate the query with a customer and authenticate the query if necessary. The QueryResult contains a character string that holds a human readable query result. This

Table 3.2: CSM message objects.

Type code	Message class	Purpose
1	Query	The customer sends this message to a CSM node to query it about the state of the node or local agents.
2	QueryResult	The node uses this object to answer a query.
3	ExecutionRequest	The customer sends this message to the node to request the execution of an agent. The message contains the bytecode of the agent and a filter describing the IP traffic the agent wishes to monitor.
4	Acknowledgement	The node sends this object to acknowledge that an agent has been started. It also uses this object to deny access to the node. It then includes a short message as to why the execution was denied.
5	Result	This message is sent from the node to the home application of the customer. It contains results the agent has calculated at that node.
7	CallBack	The node sends this message to a customer's home application to inform it that an agent likes to send results.
8	Routing Update	A node sends this message to another node to inform it about neighbor nodes.

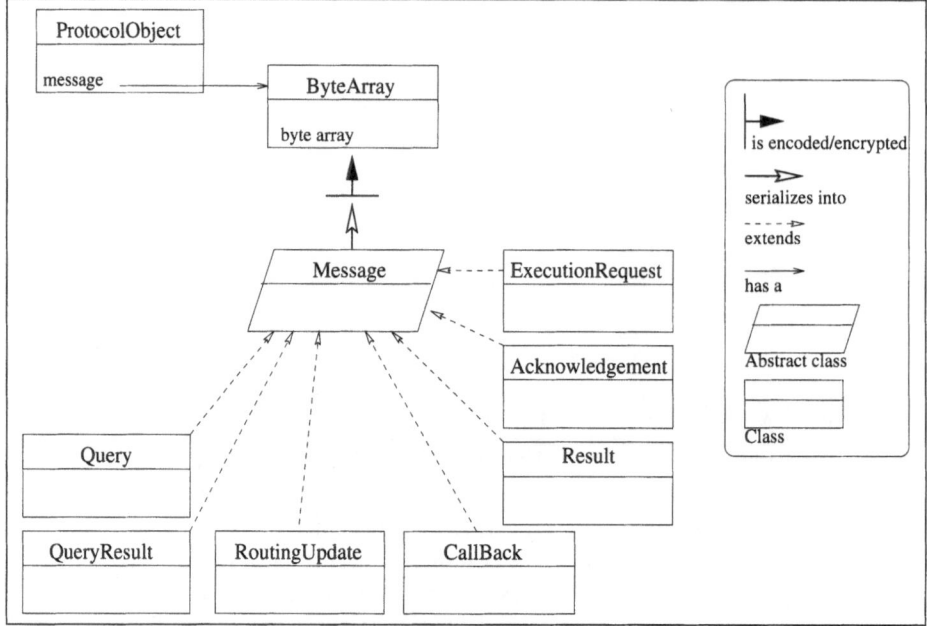

Figure 3.2: The protocol object and the message objects.

is sufficient because queries are intended for the human operators of the customer home application. The character string of an answer can simply be written into a Graphical User Interface (GUI) window. Nevertheless, the query classes can be extended to provide machine parsable answers if there is a need for doing so. Here are the currently supported query types:

- **Agent places.** Allow the customer to query about how many agents can run in a node and how many of these agent places are currently free.

- **Agent state.** This query lets the customer know which of his/her agents are currently running on a node and some performance statistics of the agents, such as how many packet they have consumed and how long they have been running so far.

- **Node policy.** The node answers with a report of the policy that is applied to the contacting customer's agents. This includes, for instance, what filters will apply (see section 2.3.3), the maximum total CPU time an agent can use, and the transmission rate that the node provides to an agent.

- **Node services.** Provides a list of the services that an agent can request from a node together with a short description of each service (see section 3.3.4).

- **Neighbors.** This query delivers contact information, such as IP addresses and port numbers of neighbor nodes of the queried node.

- **Routing.** The customer can ask the node as to what node it would route an agent that is heading for a specific IP address. This query was used for the debugging of the agent forwarding.

3.1.6   CSM Message Exchange Sequences

All CSM communication is implemented using TCP connections. This is useful since the CSM protocol is not time-critical but should be reliable. The CSM client connects to the server on a well-known port. A TCP connection is only used for one transaction (complete and valid sequence of messages exchanged), thus the message objects do not have to contain a sequence number. The CSM communication transactions are grouped according to their three purposes: information of customers (queries), transfer of agents as well as agent results, and node topology administration.

Queries follow a simple pattern. The client (the home application) opens a connection to the CSM server port of a node. It sends a query object and receives a query result. Afterwards both communication parties close the connection (see figure 3.3).

For agent execution the client wraps an agent into an ExecutionRequest message. It sends this message and receives an Acknowledge message (see figure 3.3). The message contains a bit that signals whether the execution is accepted by the node or not (Nack). If the node executes the agent, it hands the open connection to the node service handler. By requesting the *result transmission* node service, the agent can now use the open connection to send an arbitrary amount of Result messages. The result message in turn can indicate if the agent wishes to close the connection. Note that the node can close the connection at any time if it detects a policy violation.

If the agent is forwarded (a node acts as a client - see section 2.4), the results of an agent cannot be sent along the connection. Else, a forwarding node would have to keep many connections open and route results of forwarded agents. Instead, agents close the connection with a dummy result and request a new connection from the local node. The node then sends a CallBack message object to the address and port provided by the agent. Again, the agent then sends its results along the open connection using the Result message objects in the same way as described earlier. Note that customers can easily introduce new result formats by subclassing `clientserver.Result`.

The RoutingUpdate message is no fundamental part of CSM communication. If a node learns about new neighbor nodes, it sends this message to all of its neighbors and then immediately closes the connection again. The CSM nodes use this one-way message to implement a node routing table (overlay topology) so that nodes can learn how to forward agents along a route towards a given IP address (see section 3.7).

3.2   The T-Component and the Raw Packet Protocol

The T-component is a packet copy mechanism integrated directly in the peering router or attached to the peering connection. The T-component provides the genericity to customer-based service monitoring. It does so by giving the customer access to any IP packet of an

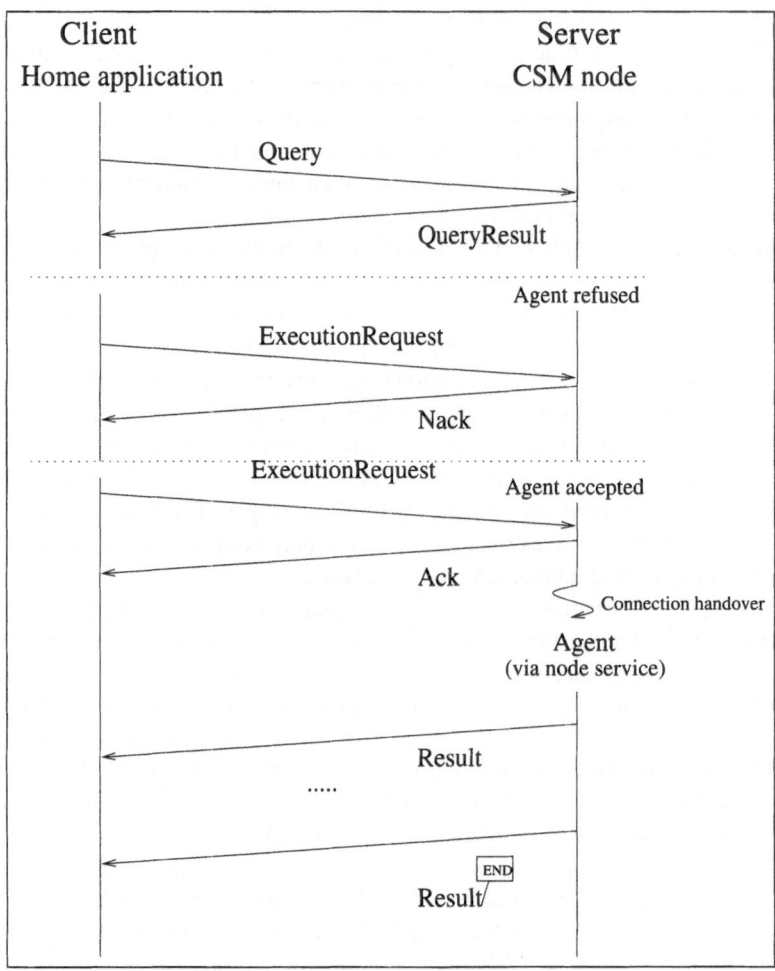

Figure 3.3: The query and the agent execution protocol.

IP service associated with that customer plus the packet's position in time and space. The CSM architecture separates the T-component from the CSM node for several reasons: the T-component must be very fast and should not interfere with the normal packet forwarding of a router. Therefore, T-components depend on the specific architecture of the peering points. T-components will meet these requirements best if they are directly integrated by the network equipment manufacturer or if they are implemented in network specific measurement hardware, such as protocol analyzers [CC98]. A T-component can also be used for other applications than just customer-based service monitoring (e.g. provider specific management software). So, because of its equipment dependence and its usefulness in other contexts it makes sense to factor out the T-component into a separate entity.

This section describes what kind of T-components have been implemented, how these T-components interact with the CSM node, and what other options exist to implement a T-component.

3.2.1 T-Component Implementations

The CSM implementation can use three kinds of T-components: an offline version that uses traffic traces stored in files, an online version that copies IP traffic from Ethernet cards in promiscuous mode and a version for virtual routers which is called *t-bone*.

The former two component versions are related to each other. Both are Unix shell scripts that start a C++ client to send the packet copies and use the Unix pipe and filters mechanism to feed the C++ client. Both T-components use the tcpdump program [JLM89]. Tcpdump is a network management tool that is normally used to print out the headers of packets on a network interface matching boolean expressions. It also supports binary traffic dumps of complete link layer packets. One T-component uses this mode together with the boolean expression to copy IP traffic. The offline version of the T-component uses tcpdump output that has been previously stored in a file while the online version starts tcpdump directly with the appropriate boolean expression.

The t-bone is a T-component for so-called virtual routers [BB00]. Virtual routers are emulations of IP routers that can run on one or more PCs. The routers can forward IP traffic generated from real world applications. The t-bone is written in C and also includes the functionality to connect to the node.

3.2.2 The Interaction between the Node and the T-component

Since the T-component is device dependent and may be realized in software or hardware, standardizing a communication protocol may not be useful. However, in order to reduce the implementation work, the communication between the node and T-component is kept simple and uniform. All three T-component versions use the same protocol to send packet copies. The protocol is called the Raw Packet Protocol. However, the T-components differ in the way in which the node requests the copies. For script-based T-components the node starts a new T-component for each request. It passes a T-component-specific filter description, an IP address, and a TCP port number as arguments to the script. Once a script-based T-component runs, it uses the port and address to open a TCP connection to the node. Then it starts sending the copied packets. The T-component for the virtual router is more convenient. The node simply connects to the T-component and requests the packets. The T-component then sends the packets via the already open connection.

Request for IP packet copies.   The node contains an object of the class node.T_Configurator which is able to order packet copies from T-components or to start T-components if needed. As mentioned before two of the available T-components are scripts. The configurator starts the offline T-component with a file name as argument along with the port and address for the callback. The online version also obtains the boolean filter expression for the tcpdump program. The configurator calculates this expression from the filter that the node generated for the agent (see section 2.3.3). Therefore, only packets are sent that the agent has requested and that are allowed to be seen by the agent. In case the node is not located on the machine to be monitored, the script is started remotely using UNIX's rsh command. Note that each agent receives its packet copies on a separate connection. This improves the CSM performance since the demultiplexing of packet copies would impose additional workload on the node which could then become a bottleneck. Additionally, when using scripted T-components, each agent leads to the start of a T-component. This is not the case for the t-bone, the T-component of the virtual routers. Instead, the t-bone is started as an attached program to a virtual router. The t-bone includes a TCP server accepting requests for IP packet copies. A request consists of a human readable ASCII string terminated by the end-of-line character. The syntax and semantics is not described in detail here, because it is device specific. Take a look at this illustrating example instead, which orders the next 100 packets of TCP traffic coming from the subnet 10 and going to the subnet 11.12.13:

```
gimme -number 100 -src 10.10.10.10/8 -dst 11.12.13.14/24 -proto 6
```

Keep in mind that the t-bone's server is reentrant, meaning it can handle several node requests at the same time.

Delivery of the IP packet copies: the raw packet protocol.   All T-components send the packets on an open TCP connection according to the raw packet format. The format has a fixed header of 10 bytes followed by a variable payload part that contains a copy of one IP packet. As long as the T-component copies packets, it keeps sending a header followed by a variable part. The protocol finishes when either the node or the T-component closes the TCP connection. The header uses little-endian numbers. The first two bytes encode the length of the payload in bytes. This reflects the possible length of the encapsulated IP packet. Note that we cannot use the length field of the IP packet since the T-component may already have truncated the payload according to the filter it has received from the node. The other eight bytes of the header encode a time stamp. The timestamp stores the time that has passed between January 1, 1970, and the arrival of the packet. The first four bytes encode the seconds, whereas the second 4 bytes encode the micro seconds.

3.2.3 Other Options for T-components

The T-component is device specific and this influences also the way the node has to request packet copies. In this section we discuss alternatives on how the T-component can be implemented, focusing on how the packet copies can be acquired in a non-intrusive way. We differ between an approach using additional hardware, one applying additional functionality provided in network hardware, and a software-based approach.

Protocol analyzer hardware. As said before, the T-component may acquire the packet copies from a protocol analyzer [CC98]. Protocol analyzers are instruments dedicated to analyze a communication protocol. Protocol analyzers are used to troubleshoot network problems and to monitor network performance. The analyzer has built-in knowledge of the protocol to ease the analysis (e.g. for Ethernet or for ATM). Nevertheless, a protocol analyzer has the capability of passive traffic recording, and therefore it can be used as a T-component. Often traffic analyzers are portable devices with dedicated hardware and high performance. However, they are usually expensive. Also, they provide far more functionality than needed for a T-component. Finally, there is no standardized interface to control protocol analyzers remotely.

Enhanced network devices. The Simple Network Management Protocol (SNMP) [CFSD90, Sta99] is an Internet standard protocol to manage and monitor network devices. Network state information is structured in Management Information Bases (MIB). If the peering device fully supports the Remote Network Monitoring MIB (RMON) [Wal95, Wal97], it can act as a T-component. RMON defines objects of a so-called *filter group* that allows the CSM filtering and objects in a so-called *packet capture group* which can be used as the CSM packet copy mechanism (see section 6.2.2). Unfortunately most router manufacturers do not fully support the packet capture mechanism. Cisco, for example, only supports the capture of packet headers [Cis00a]. For testing purposes, however, we used the port-redirection mechanism [Cab98] (which is a subset of the packet capture group) of Cabletron's SmartSwitch to feed a T-component.

Packet capture software. Modern operating systems allow personal computers to act as routers. They also provide libraries to capture and copy routed network traffic. For example, libcap is a packet capture library for Unix systems [MJ93]. On Win32 platforms the NDIS packet capture library is included. Developers can use these libraries to implement network measurement applications (e.g. [DS00]) and, of course, to implement a T-component. However, the performance of a software solution depends on the implementation of the library, the speed of the host machine, and on the operating system.

3.3 The CSM Node

This section describes the CSM node implementation, which is a central part of the CSM implementation. The node is divided into four functional parts: CSM communication, agent management, node topology, and configuration. This chapter will not list all classes involved because a lot of that material is not relevant for CSM. Instead it will focus on the important features, such as agent execution, node services, and overall design.

3.3.1 Node Overview

Figure 3.4 shows a simplified object hierarchy of a running node. A node is started by creating a node object. The node object has to set up a number of helper objects from different packages and to provide the node functionality. This subsection briefly explains the most important ones. The node uses helper objects from the `config` package to learn about its basic configuration, such as its unique name, node resource limits (e.g. number of agent places), the location as well as the type of T-component to be used, and other configuration sources, e.g. additional file paths and names. The `config` package was factored out because it can also be used by the home application. This is also true for the `topology` packet. This packet includes classes that can provide a name service, a neighboring service, and a routing service to the node. The name service is used to map a node name to an IP address and port number. The neighboring service consults a configuration file to provide names of neighbor nodes. The routing service includes a client-server functionality (using the CSM protocol) to dynamically establish a routing table for forwarding agents from node to node. The node has a server receiving queries or agent execution requests via the CSM protocol (see section 3.1). Arriving CSM requests are delegated to appropriate handlers. Another important node object is the Registry. It registers agents and manages the available resources. The registry is responsible for the admission control. It associates agents with users and attaches individual policies to the agents. The registry deduces the policies from user profiles stored in a file. The registry also has a ResourceController object which dynamically checks the resource consumption of the agents. The registry stores handles to the running agents and to their execution environments.

3.3.2 Welcome Procedure for an Agent

A customer request for the execution of an agent first arrives at the server, which starts a new thread to handle the request. The request then passes through the CSM protocol stack (see section 3.1.3). The stack delivers an ExecutionRequest to the ExecutionRequestHandler along with information whether the agent has been encrypted and successfully authenticated. The handler will now register the agent and prepare the execution environment for the agent before it finally starts the agent. The procedure will follow in more detail hereafter. Note that each step can fail, in which case the sender of the agent receives a negative Acknowledgement message containing an error description (see section 3.1.5). The handler also resets allocations for the agent made in earlier steps.

1. The handler contacts the registry to obtain a policy for the agent. The registry uses the sender and the authentication information to determine the appropriate policy. It can also entirely reject the agent.

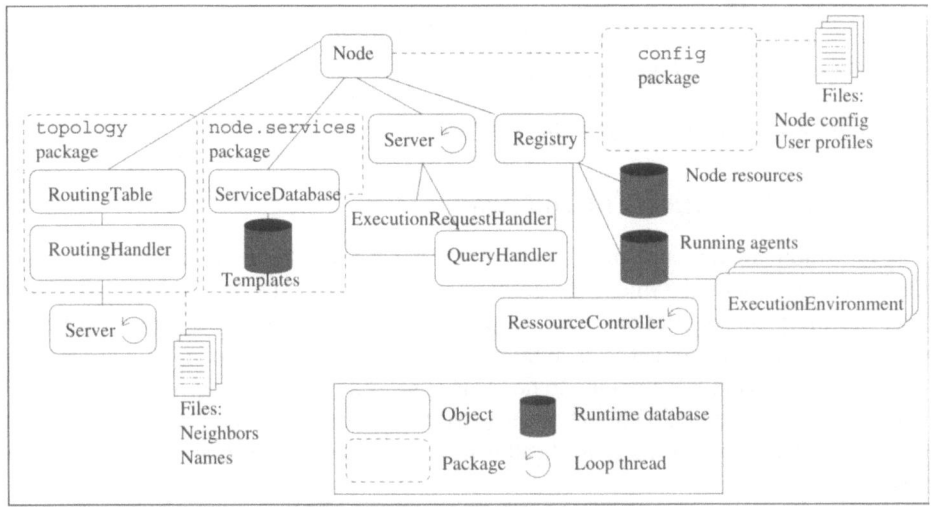

Figure 3.4: Node implementation overview.

2. The handler instantiates the agent object using the AgentClassLoader. This class-loader can create an Agent object from an ExecutionRequest message (containing Java bytecode).

3. The handler creates the filter to be applied to the agent by cutting the requested filter (in the ExecutionRequest object) with the filter of the policy (see section 2.3.3).

4. The handler starts preparing the execution environment for the agent. If the T-component uses a callback mechanism (see section 3.2.2), the handler allocates a port for that purpose. It also instantiates the execution environment components and queues (see section 3.3.3).

5. The handler instantiates an ExecutionEnvironment which is a container for all objects that are part of the execution environment.

6. The handler instantiates a RessourceUsage object that holds references to the ExecutionEnvironment and that is used to account the resource usage by the agent.

7. The handler registers the agent at the Registry. This may fail if, for example, a run-time resource over-usage has occurred (see section 3.5).

8. The agent is initialized to prepare it for the reception of monitored traffic.

9. The handler now starts the execution environment. First it installs the node services. Then the node service handler, the agent wrapper (that feeds the agent) and the receiver of the raw packet protocol (see section 3.2.2) is started (in this order). Each is running in a separate thread.

10. The T_configurator is started to start/connect to the T-component.

11. The forwarding of the agent is triggered (if requested).

12. The agent is acknowledged via the CSM protocol.

3.3.3 The Execution Environment

The execution environment encapsulates an agent. It protects the node from the agent, forwards the monitored traffic to the agent and serves the agent's service requests. It also accounts every operation of the agent. A specialty of the proposed CSM node architecture is that the agent does not get its own thread. Instead the agent is invoked by the environment whenever there is something to do. This approach increases security and makes resource accounting easier. Although the approach introduces a performance overhead due to thread context switches, the overhead is not a bottleneck of the CSM implementation (see chapter 5).

The execution environment mainly consists of subclasses of the abstract class node.EnvironmentComponents. Figure 3.5 shows the inheritance graph for the execution environment components.

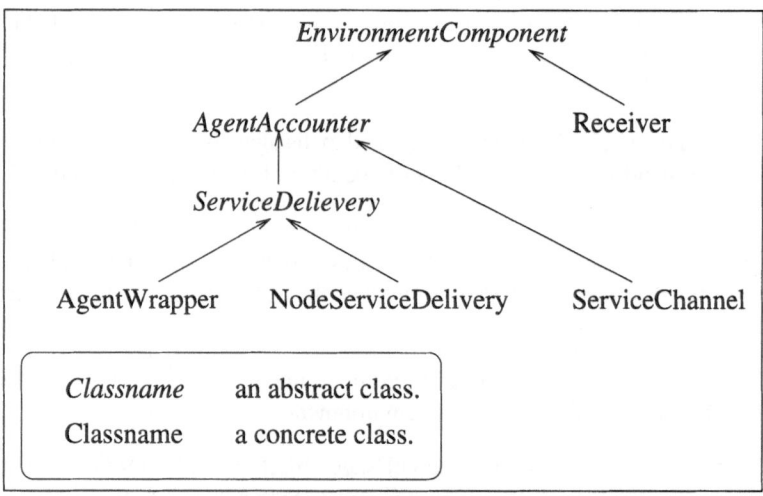

Figure 3.5: Execution environment inheritance graph.

All EnvironmentComponents encapsulate and run in their own thread. The thread management functionality is implemented in this abstract superclass. The AgentAccounter contains functionality to record the running time of a single method of an agent. The ServiceChannel handles service requests of the agent (see section 3.3.4). The abstract ServiceDelivery class implements functionality to call methods of the agent, thus to start agent behavior. The objects of (sub)class ServiceDelivery are the only objects of the node that call methods of the CSM agent. Two classes use that functionality: on the one hand, the AgentWrapper delivers the monitored IP packets to the agent by calling a method of the agent and passing an object of class IPPacket to the method. On the other hand, the NodeServiceDelivery also uses a method call to the agent to deliver a result of a service requested by the agent.

Figure 3.6 shows the internals of an execution environment. The Receiver obtains the monitored IP packets from the T-component via the raw packet protocol. It creates an IPPacket object of each received packet and puts it in an ObjectQueue. The AgentWrapper (running in a separate thread) afterwards grabs the packet and hands it to the agent via a method call. For accounting purposes the wrapper measures the execution time of the method call. Note that each agent's reaction to the monitoring of an IP packet runs in the thread of the AgentWrapper. The agent can calculate its measurements on the packet, store temporary results, and request node services by placing a Service object in the ObjectQueue of the ServiceChannel. One important service of the node is to send back an agent result to the home application. Some services put a reply to the service invocation into the queue of the ServiceDelivery. The delivery of this reply proceeds similar to the delivery of monitored packets. Keep in mind that the execution environment architecture completely separates the agent from the rest of the node. The only object reference a node object that the agent has is the reference to a ServiceChannel. There the only method the agent can call is the put (Service service) to request a node service. Furthermore, the agent can only run when it is called. Note that the AgentWrapper and the NodeServiceDelivery are quite similar. In fact, a design alternative would only provide the ServiceDelivery. An additional node service would then be that the agent can request monitored packets. This would simplify the design. However, the agent would have to demultiplex service replies that are monitored IP packets and other service replies. Since usually the node services are used only now and then, but monitored IP packets may come in fast, in bursts, and must be handled as fast as possible, the author decided to provide a separate lane for the monitored packets. Also, the mentioned duplication of functionality did not result in duplicated code since the implementation factors out the common functionalities of the AgentWrapper and the NodeServiceDelivery into the common superclasses (see figure 3.5).

3.3.4 Node Services

Running agents have only one object reference to the execution environment, and this is a reference to the ServiceChannel where they can place requests for node services. The classes that support node services are bundled in the a sub-package of the node named node.services. To request a service, the Agent creates a Service object and puts it into the queue (see figure 3.6). Some services generate one or more replies that are delivered back to the agent by the NodeServiceDelivery object of the execution environment. Note that the delivery is asynchronous, it takes place via a queue. The class Service is defined as follows:

```
public class Service {
    protected static long current=0;
```

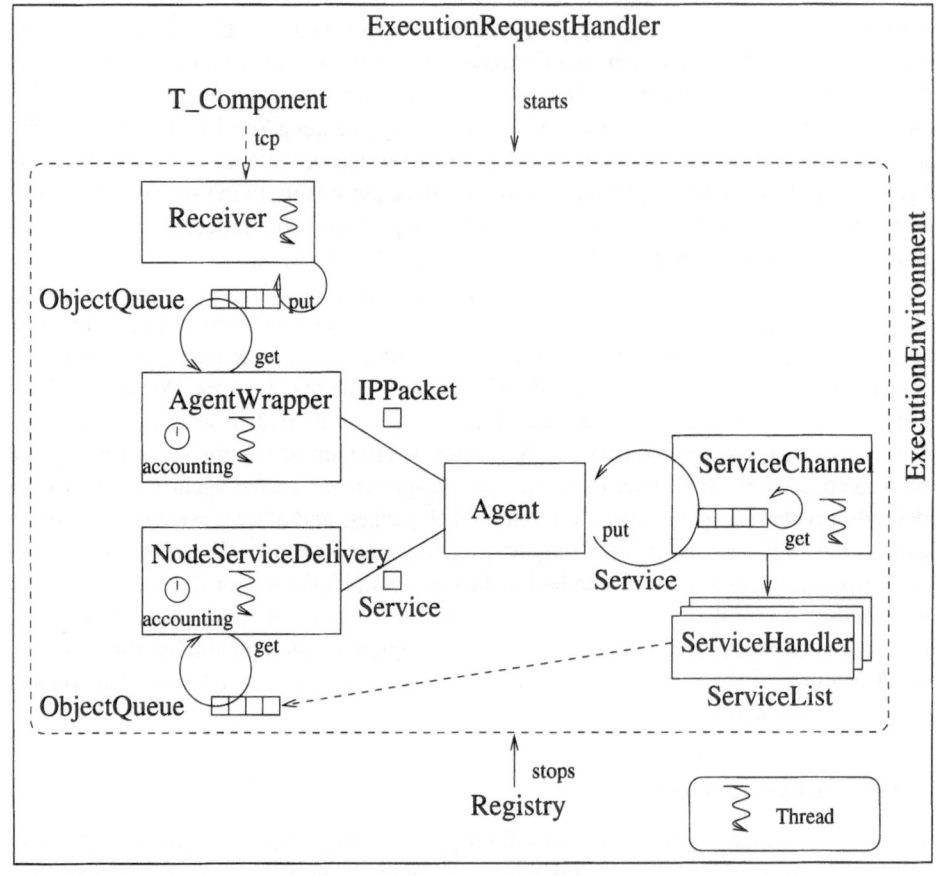

Figure 3.6: Execution environment.

```
protected long number;
protected int type;
protected java.util.Vector args;
```

`...`

`}`

Each service request is numbered (instance variable `number`). The (static) class variable `current` helps to guarantee the uniqueness of the number. The `type` field identifies the desired service. Different services may need different kinds and numbers of arguments. The built-in Java class `java.util.Vector` is a container of an arbitrary number of arbitrary Java objects. A vector is thus the ideal type for the `args` instance variable which has to store the arguments for all kinds of service requests. Replies to the service are also delivered in objects of class Service. The type and number field of these objects allow the agent to map a service reply to the request that triggered the reply. In the reply the arguments hold results or status messages of the reply.

The ServiceChannel removes service requests from the queue. It has a ServiceList that stores references to a handler for each service type. The ServiceChannel calls the appropriate handler and passes the service request to it. The ServiceHandler then executes the service operations. It also deposits results (if there are some) in the reply queue. The service channel and all service handlers can terminate the agent if the agent requests services without permission or if a serious exception occurs during delivery of the service. The ServiceDatabase stores templates of service handlers. When the execution environment of an agent is constructed (see section 3.3.2), the service list for the agent is constructed from the templates in the database according to the policy valid for the agent in question.

Supported node services. Here is a list of the node services that the CSM node implementation supports, along with a short description of the service, its arguments, and its reply behavior:

- **Self-termination.** As mentioned before, the agent has no thread of its own. Instead it is invoked by the execution environment every time there is something to do. If the agent wishes to stop these invocations, it calls this service. The node will then deallocate the execution environment and de-register (thus kill) the agent. The self-termination service request has no argument and will trigger no reply to the agent.

- **Result transmission.** The agent can request to send a result object along its open connection. This is the most important node service since it is the only way how the agent can deliver monitoring results to the customer. The open connection that is used for the transmission is usually the one that the agent was delivered on. The service object must contain an object of class `clientserver.Result` as argument (see CSM communication in section 3.1). CSM communication is reliable, and therefore the agent does not get a reply.

- **Host information.** This service provides the agent with general information about the host that executes it. Thus, forwarded agents can check themselves if they monitor traffic at interesting locations. This service request has no arguments. The reply contains three arguments: the name (identifier) of the node, the name of the organization owning the node, and the DNS address of the node. These names are encoded as Java character strings.

- **Timer.** Since agents are only invoked when something (e.g. a monitored packet) is delivered, an agent cannot perform tasks based on regular time intervals or time-outs. Consider an agent that measures the load of a service not in use. If no packet is monitored, the agent stays passive and cannot report that the service is not used. To alleviate this shortcoming the CSM nodes offer a timer service. This service delivers a reply to the agent every x jiffies[1] for n times. The agent uses two integer numbers as arguments in the request, namely x and n. Each of the n replies will 'wake up' the agent and allow it to e.g. send a report message. The replies contain an integer number that simply contains the reply number.

- **Change the connection.** This service closes the currently open connection and tries to open a new one. This service is important for forwarded agents since these do not have an open connection to their home application. The agent must provide several arguments in the request: a character string for the DNS name of the receiver, an integer number for the port, two boolean values that indicate if the node should encrypt and authenticate the connection, respectively, and, if so, a character string with the identity of the receiving party (used for PGP cryptography). The service handler then disconnects the current connection and tries to establish the new connection. The service reply contains a boolean indicating if the connection was established. In order to send by means of the new connection, the agent simply uses the result transmission service.

- *Stop all agents.* This service stops all running agents and deallocates their execution environment. It thus resets the node. This is a privileged service that only authenticated and authorized agents can execute. It takes no argument and does not invoke a reply.

- *Stop the node.* This service leads to the graceful termination of the complete CSM node. This is a privileged service that only authenticated and authorized agents can carry out. It takes no argument and does not invoke a reply.

Note that the first five services are considered to be standard and are provided to all agents. The last two service need explicit permission by the policy (see section 3.3.5).

---

[1] Here, a jiffy is equivalent to 100 milliseconds.

They are useful to manage the CSM nodes. Some interesting but unimplemented node services are described in section 4.5.2.

Security of node services. The node services allow the agent to perform actions that are otherwise forbidden and prevented. The agent cannot, for example, open a socket. The security manager would terminate the agent for trying this operation (see section 3.5). Node services provide access to dangerous functionality in a controlled way. Each agent is associated with a policy that exclusively describes what services are delivered to that agent (see next section). If the agent requests other services or does not provide proper arguments, it is killed immediately. The node policy can also mark some services as privileged services. The node stopping service can, for example, only be triggered by an agent that was authenticated as being sent by a super user of the node. The ServiceHandler accounts the service execution time. This helps to prevent node service based denial-of-service attacks by the agents. Furthermore, each service handler can restrict the number of consecutive service requests. The timer service can, for instance, only be called once. All node services are designed to execute quickly and to use little node resources. The timer service, for example, uses a large minimum time between two wake-ups. The change-channel and sending service enforce that only one connection per agent can be open at any time.

Additional node services. Of course, one may imagine many more useful node services. One service, for example, could be the migration of an agent. An agent could request that it will be sent to another node. It could also request that its state be preserved (strong migration [SBB+00, BLP00]). Yet, none of the CSM applications described in chapter 4 needs strong mobility. So this is not a supported feature of the CSM node implementation. Instead, agent forwarding is used (see section 2.4). However, if a new node service, such as strong migration, will become necessary, adding a new service is no problem. The CSM node developer simply has to provide a new template for the service handler (a subclass of ServiceHandler), which implements the service and then add it to the service database.

3.3.5 User Profiles and Policies

Each agent has an individual policy attached to its execution environment. The policy is individually calculated by the Registry during the welcome procedure of the agent (see section 3.3.2). While the execution environment is set up, the environment components access the policy information relevant to them. Then the components can enforce the policy directly. Other objects, such as the resource controller (see section 3.5), also access the policy throughout the lifetime of an agent.

The Policy. Policy objects represent agent resource limits and authorization during the lifetime of an agent. Here is the interface (the public methods) of the Policy class:

```
public interface Policy {
    public Filter
      getFirstMatchingFilter(filter.Filter requested);
    public boolean mustAuthenticate();
    public boolean isSuperUser();
    public long maxExecTime();
    public long maxMem();
    public int time2live();
    public short priority();
    public Vector services();
}
```

The getFirstMatchingFilter() method takes the filter requested by the agent and returns the filter that will finally apply to the agent. This method implements the filter policy. The registry uses this method to learn the filter to be used when installing the filtering of monitored IP packets. The mustAuthenticate() method indicates if the agent associated with that policy must authenticate itself with cryptographic means. The isSuperUser() method tells if the agent associated with that policy is sent by a super user. The maxExecTime(), maxMem(), and time2live() methods provide policy information about limits to the run-time resource consumption. The priority() method returns the priority of the agent. These methods are used by the resource controller. The services() method returns a list of node service types that the agent is allowed to request.

User profile. In order to associate a policy to an agent, the registry consults the user database (see figure 3.4 in section 3.3.1) to retrieve a user profile. The user profile stores a user ID (that is necessary for cryptography), network addresses administered by that user, the kind of policy applied to the agents of that user, and the type numbers of additional node services granted to the user in question. Table 3.3 illustrates how a user profile database may look like. The first two profiles are normal customers. The third one is a super user. The last one is an anonymous user. The anonymous user is not associated with any IP subnet. The CSM node implementation stores the user profile in a file.

Table 3.3: User profiles.

Node ID	Networks	Policy group	Services
admin@iam.unibe.ch	130.92	CustomerPolicyGen	
admin@cui.unige.ch	129.194.90	CustomerPolicyGen	
root@iam.unibe.ch	130.92 129.194.90	SuperPolicyGen	555 666
anonymous		AnonymUserPolicyGen	

Policy Generators.   The user profile describes what kind of policy is attached to agents of that user. The description may be complex, so it is not defined in a data structure but instead stored in a separate class. Therefore, policies can, for example, use different procedures to calculate the filters. This would not be possible with (passive) typed data. However, introducing a policy class per customer would not be a very scalable solution. Instead, CSM uses policy generators. A policy generator abstracts a group of similar policies. At run time it generates policy objects of that group. The example profiles in table 3.3 refer to three kinds of policy generators. One functionality of the policy is that it limits the filters an agent can request. The CustomerPolicyGenerator creates policies that use the cut mechanism (see section 2.3.3) to permit only the monitoring of traffic that originates from or goes to IP addresses associated with the customer. The SuperPolicyGen creates a policy that allows arbitrary monitoring. The AnonymousUserPolicy creates a policy permitting only monitoring of packet headers or of encrypted traffic. On the other hand the agents under the AnonymousUserPolicy policies do not have to be authenticated. Note that the introduction of new policies is simple. You only have to generate a subclass of Policy that implements e.g. the filter cut mechanism the way you want. Then, you have to create a subclass of `PolicyGenerator` that calculates and creates (possibly using the user profile) a policy object with the behavior of your choice.

Figure 3.7 gives an overview of the use of policies, policy generators, and user profiles.

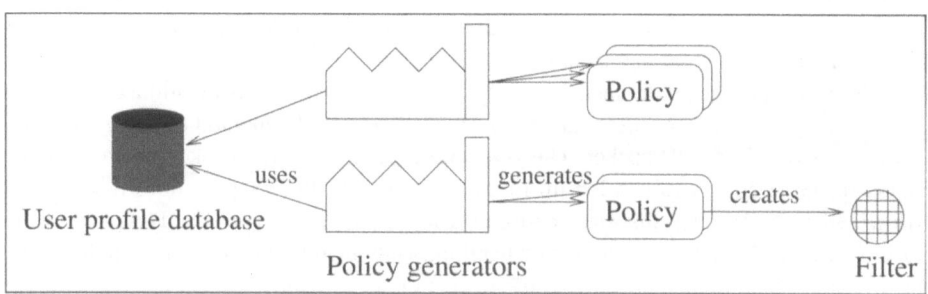

Figure 3.7: Overview of policy, policy generators and user profiles.

3.4   Agent Interface

This section describes what the CSM node knows about the agent. It does not present the implemented agents. They will be presented in chapter 4. ¿From what has been discussed in section 3.1.2, we know that the classloader needs an interface declaration or an abstract class description of the class that implements the customer agent. Note that this is not necessary for the helper classes that the agents' byte code may bring with it. The helper classes are only used by the agent itself, so the hosting environment (the node) does not have to know about them.

CSM defines an interface that must be implemented by all CSM agents in order to be executed in CSM nodes. Here follows the interface declaration of the agent:

```
(1)  package capsule;
(2)  public interface Agent extends java.io.Serializable {
(3)     public void handlePacket (node.IPPacket p);
(4)     public void handleService (node.services.Service s );
(5)     public void emergencyHandle(node.IPPacket p);
(6)     public boolean init(java.util.Vector initVector);
(7)     public void stop();
(8)     public void putServiceChannel(node.ServiceChannel s);}
```

Line (1) says that the agent interface declaration is located in a separate package called capsule. The separation is used to ease source code management at the customer side of the application where hundreds of agents may be implemented. The name of the package comes from the active networking background of the CSM application where a capsule is an executable network packet. Line (2) starts the interface declaration. Note that for resource management the agent must be serializable (see sections 3.1.2 and 3.5). The lines (3-8) declare the public methods an agent must implement. As mentioned in section 3.3.3, the AgentWrapper object calls the handlePacket () method of an agent to deliver a new monitored IP packet. The AgentWrapper obtains the packets from a queue. If the queue is almost full (filled up to e.g. 80 percent), the wrapper does not call the handlePacket () but the emergencyHandle () method (line 5). The exact value of the fill level that triggers emergency handling is defined by the local node policy. The agent should thus implement handlePacket () as a method for fast packet handling in case of congestion. This reduces the risk for the agent that it will be killed by the node because of a full queue (see section 3.5). The handleService () method is called by the ServiceDelivery object to deliver a reply to a node service request. The init () method is called after the agent has been instantiated but before monitored packets are delivered. Thus, the agent gets a chance to prepare itself for the packet handling. The init method uses a java.util.Vector object as a generic container for an arbitrary number of initialization arguments. The method returns a message whether the initialization was successful. If not, the agent is stopped. The stop () method is called when the agent is to be stopped gracefully. This, for instance, happens when the upper limit of packets to be delivered is reached. In the stop method the agent can, for example, implement the sending of a final report to the home application. The putServiceChannel () method is only called once, during the initialization procedure of the agent, in order to connect the agent to the service channel. The service channel is the only way the agent can communicate with the node and with the rest of the world.

3.5 Security and Resource Control

3.5.1 Communication Protection

The CSM protocol implementation (see section 3.1) provides the capability to encrypt and authenticate messages using the Pretty Good Privacy program (PGP 2.6.3i). This PGP version encrypts with the International Data Encryption Algorithm (IDEA) [Lai92] using a 128 bit session key. The protection of the key exchange and the signature is supported by the RSA algorithm [RSA78] using a 1024 bit key pair. The CSM protocol supports three modes: plain text, encrypted and signed, and signed-only. When the client contacts a server in a certain mode, the server always replies in that same mode. Thus, when the customer sends an encrypted agent, the results to be sent back are also encrypted by the node. Agents that use the call-back can request the mode that the node should use. Therefore, intermediate providers cannot access encrypted results that an agent sends back to the home application unless the providers conspire. So, all CSM protocol actions (e.g. agent sending, result reception, queries, etc.) can be protected, if desired, against man-in-the-middle attacks. Note that currently only PGP-based protection is implemented. Yet, the CSM protocol can easily be extended to use other cryptography packages.

The regular IP traffic flow must be protected from the monitoring agents. The node does so by applying a policy that controls the filtering. The policy uses filters to describe what kind of traffic an agent may monitor and how much of that traffic can be seen by the agent (see section 2.3.3). If a provider does not install the proper filtering policies, the agents may be granted access to other customers' traffic. However, this is also the case today. The next section describes why an agent cannot circumvent the node policy mechanism, such as the filtering.

3.5.2 Security Layers of the Node

The node encapsulates the running agents in sandboxes to deprive them from any possibility of manipulating the node or other agents. The execution environment of the agent is its sandbox. It exposes only a reference to one single object, namely the ServiceChannel. Java offers protection mechanisms for class methods. A method can be declared accessible by either objects of that class only, or by objects of subclasses only, or by objects of classes in the same package or by any object. The CSM implementation isolates the agent classes in a package of its own and uses this mechanism to protect all methods of the ServiceChannel so that the agent can only access one method. The method simply places a service request into a queue (see section 3.3.4), so it cannot be misused for an attack. This very method on one object reference is the agent's only access point to the node. The agent does not have a thread of its own either. It completely depends on the computation time of the threads of its execution environment. Note that these threads run with a relatively low priority. The CSM node uses its own Java security manager to prevent illegal resource access by the node.

The Security Manager. Java uses a security manager to lock loaded code into a conceptual sand-box. The security manager is an integrated part of Java's class loading mechanism. The security manager keeps track of classes which are loaded from external sources (not by the default class loader). CSM agents are instantiated from external sources, namely by the AgentClassLoader that instantiates the agent from the CSM message object (see section 3.1.2). The security manager checks each invocation of a security critical method. It analyzes the method call stack to see if loaded code has been involved in the method call. If yes, the security manager interrupts the invocation by throwing a security exception. While Java's security managers form a nice concept, the definition of a new security manager is relatively tedious. For every security critical method, the developer must write a check routine. The CSM node implementation uses an extension of the `java.rmi.RMISecurityManager` class. This class defines a very restrictive security policy. No loaded code is allowed to access the file system, any thread control or the network[2].

3.5.3   Resource Control

The CSM sand-box prevents the agent from carrying out an illegal operation. However, the agent may excessively use legal operations to disrupt the smooth operation of the node. This is called a denial-of-service attack against the node resources. The CSM node detects these attacks with a resource controller. The controller runs in its own thread which is set to the highest priority so that it preempts any agent activity. The controller checks in regular intervals the resource consumption of all agents. If an agent launches a denial-of-service attack against a node resource, the controller will detect it and can immediately terminate the agent. The controller uses the accounting information that the execution environment collects of each agent (see section 3.3.3).

Here follows an explanation on how the three node resources, CPU time, memory as well as network capacity, are protected.

CPU time. The AgentAccounter components of the execution environment (see section 3.3.3) provide the resource usage statistics of each agent. The resource controller uses that data and checks for each agent if:

- The agent's maximum lifetime in the node has expired.

- The agent's CPU time sums up to a value greater than a maximum threshold.

- If there was an agent method invocation that did not return within an upper limit of time.

The resource controller kills the agent if any of these conditions are true. The resource controller also checks if the node is congested. It measures this by comparing how

---

[2]If an agent wants to send something over the network, it needs to put a result transmission service request in the node service queue.

the work of each agent progresses. If one of these two conditions is met, the node is congested:

- An in-queue of an agent is full.

- In too many cases[3], an agent had to treat a monitoring packet with the emergency method (see section 3.4).

Both conditions show when at least one agent is too slow to perform its work. Then, the resource controller declares the node to be congested. During congestion, no new agent is granted admission to the node. The controller also starts the congestion resolution algorithm that determines the agent with the lowest priority and the least effective CPU resource consumption (since the last check) and terminates it:

1. Consider only agents that have executed in this checking interval. Let their execution time in the last interval be c.

2. Consider only those agents with the lowest present priority. This prevents many fast and low priority agents from being able to kill one high priority agent.

3. Find among those agents the one with the least effective CPU usage. Consider therefore the number of packets n that the T-component has captured for the agent during the last checking interval. Consider the number of packets h that the agent has handled in the interval. The kill ranking r of an agent is then $r = cn/h$. If n is zero then also h is zero and the ranking is defined to be c. If $h = 0$ then h is set to one. Note that these cases can happen, for example, if the agent does not receive packets but instead gets a reply from a node service. The agent with the highest ranking will then be killed.

The motivation of the definition of r is as follows: if the CPU time c is large or if an agent receives many packets (large n), it uses more resources. If it treats few packets (if h is small), the agent is working inefficiently. In fact, r is an estimation of the CPU time that the agent would have needed to treat all n packets delivered to it. So r reflects how greedy the agent is.

Note that the thresholds and maximum values used for resource control can be configured individually by each node.

Memory protection. The agents can create and store as many helper objects as they want. An agent could use this to launch a denial-of-service attack against the memory of the host machine. The resource controller regularly checks the size of an agent. Unfortunately, the Java virtual machine does not provide a `sizeof` primitive to do so. Instead, CSM nodes make use of the fact that agents are serializable (see sections 3.1.2 and 3.4). The controller serializes the controlled agent into a byte stream. The size of this stream is measurable and is used as an approximation of the true memory consumption of the agent.

---

[3]This is a configurable threshold of the node.

If the size exceeds a limit, the agent will be killed. The serialization is an expensive operation (see section 5.1.1), so the controller only executes this check with a configurable probability.

Network resource protection.   The agents can access the network only via the node services. Therefore, there is no need to do regular checks by the resource controller. The node services can control the resource consumption directly. The service handler for the result transmission service can, for instance, include a rate control mechanism. It can impose restrictions on the rate and the size of the messages sent. These restriction may depend on whether the messages should be authenticated or encrypted. However, as we experienced in our test, the excessive use of node services always led to a poor CPU ranking. Thus the CPU control mechanism had already regulated the use of the node services, including the network resources.

3.5.4   Agent Security

In this section we discuss how the agent is protected while it resides in a node. The agent is delivered in bytecode that programs any behavior desired by the user in the user's own programming style. This obfuscates the contents of the agent but it does not protect it in a cryptographic way. The owner of the node may decompile and reverse engineer the agent to find out what the agent intends to do. The node owner can also forge agent results and send them to the home application. Section 4.4 discusses ways to make such an attack hard and to increase the chance that the attack is detected. Note, however, that the node can always launch a denial-of-service attack against the agent, meaning, it can kill the agent at any time. Nevertheless, the customer will find out about that sooner or later. If agents of many customers do not receive the service expected, some of these customers will start to prefer the services of other providers. Therefore, it is in the best interest of the provider not to attack the agents on their node platforms.

Another type of attack is when one agent tries to attack another agent. However, the same mechanisms (sand-box, resource control) that prevent the agents from attacking the node also stop them from attacking each other. The only exception are agents with high priority. When an agent of high priority congests a node, the other agents are one by one terminated. But this behavior is created deliberately. The agents of the regular customers should run with the same priority. Only agents from the provider itself (or maybe agents from VIP customers) should run with high priority. They can then accomplish tasks, such as mission-critical trouble-shooting or even node maintenance.

3.6   The Home Application

The customer uses a so-called home application to access the customer-based service monitoring infrastructure. The application allows the customer to query nodes, send agents and to receive and visualize the agent results. The home application is not fully automated like the node. Instead, it is a tool for the customer to conveniently access the

CSM infrastructure. While the implementation of the home application needs a less complicated internal logic, it faces the problem of formatting agent results for the human eye. Since CSM agents may measure all kinds of service and network parameters, it is not possible to implement a solution that supports every view on results that a customer can think of. Instead, the CSM implementations allows developers to easily extend the application to other data representation models.

3.6.1 Implementation Overview

Like the node implementation the implementation of the CSM home application uses the clientserver package to communicate over the Internet (see section 3.1). The main parts of the home application deal with the collection of user input and the representation of agent results in graphical user interfaces. In order to be extensible, the home application implementation is built around a framework of few classes. Figure 3.8 shows the framework.

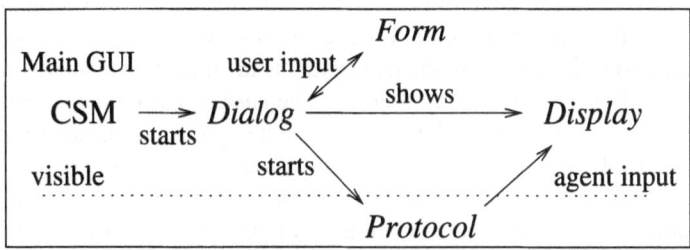

Figure 3.8: Framework of the home application.

The classes denoted as 'visual' are either extended Java abstract windowing toolkit classes or make use of them. The home application is started by instantiating an object of the main class CSM. The object displays a GUI with buttons allowing the user to start different Dialog objects, e.g. for the purpose of sending an agent or transmitting a query. Several dialogs can run concurrently. The dialogs display forms where the user can, for example, fill in what agent or query (s)he wants to send, to what node the application should send, and so on. The user can then have the dialog trigger the desired action, thereby ending the dialog. When the user applies the trigger function, the dialog also opens an independent Display object and connects it to a ProtocolObject that it has started in the background beforehand. The protocol object performs the CSM protocol transactions. It sends the appropriate CSM protocol request (e.g. an execution request to a node) and receives the answers. The protocol object forwards the answers to the displayer that represents them on the screen. The framework consists of abstract classes that implement basic functionalities and the cooperation between these classes. For every class there are three different subclasses implementing the three main types of control tracks: (1) The sending and receiving of a query, (2) the sending of an agent in end-to-end mode, and (3) the sending of an agent in a forwarding mode. The latter two are related, but the display model is quite different. When using end-to-end sending the agent replies are delivered over the initial connection. When forwarding is used, several instances of the agent try to connect back to the home application. The display for results of forwarded agent thus is more complex and needs preliminary preparation (e.g. the starting of a server).

The displays use a handful of helper classes to represent, for example, IP packet contents in different ways and to represent the network topology in case of agent forwarding.

3.6.2   The Transmission of a Request to the Node

Figure 3.9 shows the CSM main GUI and the form for sending an agent. The user has selected the *send* button of the main GUI. This has started the sending dialog that now opens a form. The main GUI has a *help* and a *quit* button providing the obvious functionalities. The *query* button starts a query dialog window. Note that for each button click a new dialog is started, so it is possible to compose and send several queries and agents at the same time. The *sending form* mainly consists of two parts: the information about the agent transmission and the filter information. Here, a customer with the customer identification *demouser* wants to send an agent to the node with the identification *admin@iam.unibe.ch*. The agent is of class `capsule.VPNAgent`. The customer can browse the file system to select available agent classes. Note that the home application needs to know if this agent will send back the results with a separate callback. The rest of the form enables the customer to specify the filter describing the IP traffic that the agent should monitor. Here, all IPSec traffic (protocols 50 and 51) coming from the subnet 130.92.0.0/16 and going to the subnet 129.0.0.0/8 is monitored. The agent wants to examine 100 packets.

Figure 3.10 shows the form for a query message. Note the similarity to the first part of the sending form. This is because the forms share common helper classes.

When the user presses the *send* button on the sending form, the dialog validates the entries (e.g. it checks if the filter description is correct and if the agent bytecode is available), starts the appropriate display window (object of class `Display`) for this kind of request, and creates a `Protocol` object. The object uses a separate thread to steer the CSM protocol interaction, thereby making use of the `clientserver` package. In case of network failure it displays warning messages. The protocol (handler) object shows an alarm if results are not encoded properly, e.g. if they are not encrypted when they should. It also forwards the node replies and the agent results to the display. The display window for an agent that was sent in end-to-end mode is depicted in figure 3.11. It has a status line on the top. Here, an agent has terminated its work at a node; the connection has been closed. Below the status line there is a scrollable text window. All result objects contain a method that prints their contents to a character string. The text window uses this method to display agent results. The text window therefore provides a generic interface for the customer to inspect agent results. Here, the agent has reported the average throughput of the measured traffic (9 kilo-bits per second). It has detected a packet that does not seem to be encrypted. Note that the result object can carry IP packets. The agent used this mechanism to send the suspicious packet back to the customer. The display provides several views to inspect the packet. Here, a header summary with a

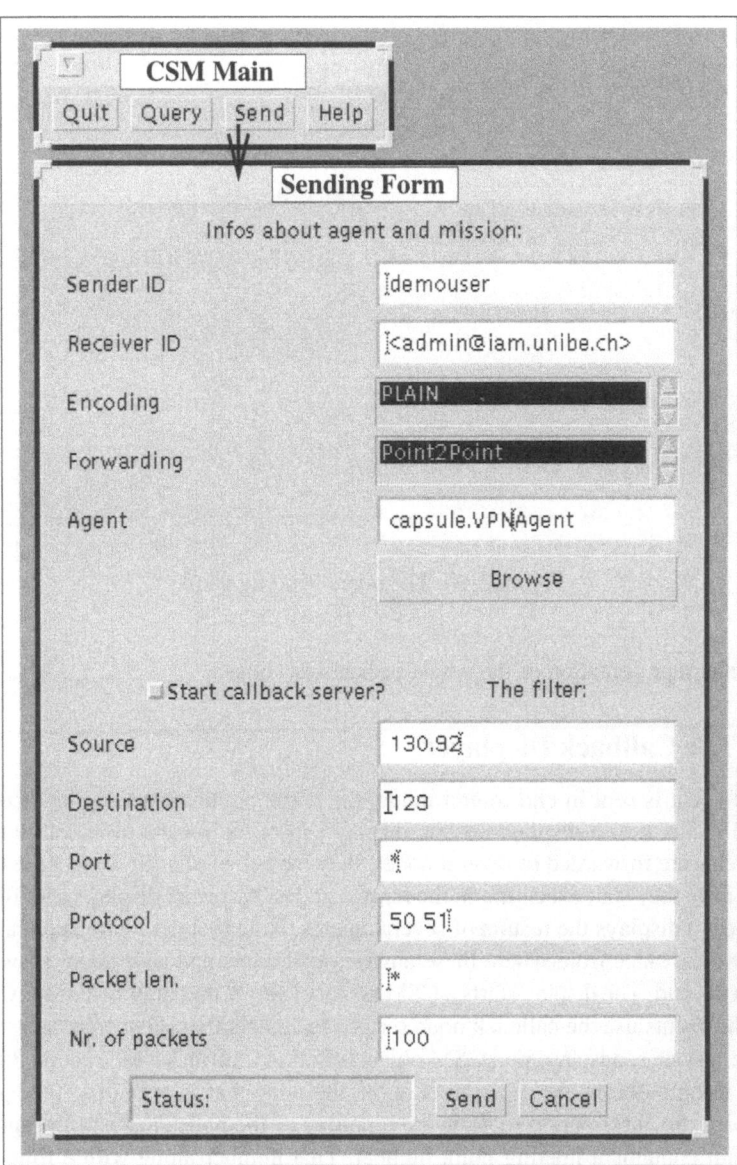

Figure 3.9: The CSM GUI and the agent sending form.

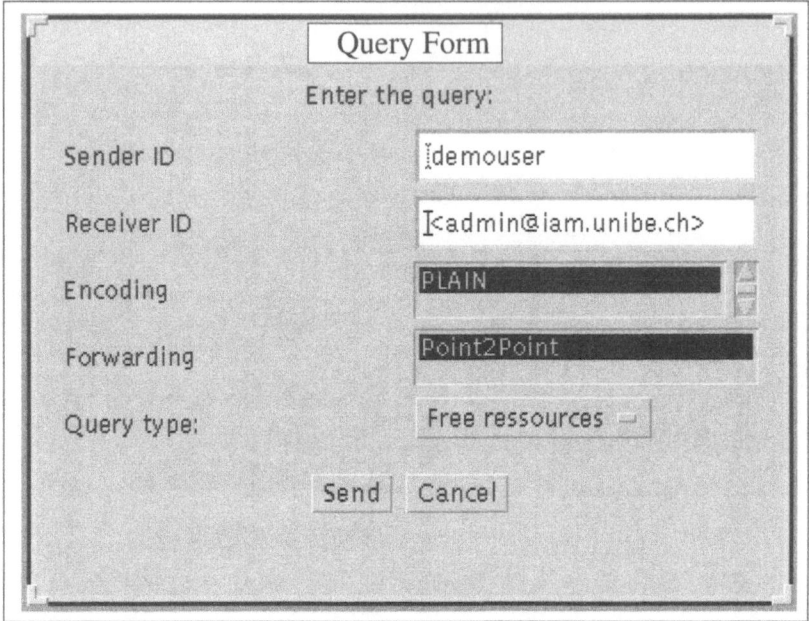

Figure 3.10: The query sending form.

hexadecimal representation of the whole packet was chosen.

3.6.3   The Callback Displayer

When an agent is sent in end-to-end mode, the home application keeps the connection open and hands it to a display. So one display shows the results of exactly one agent. When agents are forwarded to several nodes, they have to explicitly contact the home application after they start executing in the remote nodes. A special display (with the help of other objects) displays the results of several agents. Note that the home application does not know in advance from where these answers will come and how many answers there will be in the end. The display starts a CSM protocol server that only listens for CSM callbacks. The agents use the callback node service to contact that server (see section 3.3.4). The node service sends an initial CSM object (of class CallBack - see section 3.1.5). The message informs the home application about the node that is executing the agent. The display uses this information to draw the topology of the nodes that run the agent. Each agent result contains a floating point number. That number along with a time stamp is displayed close to the node where it was measured. A special value displayer performs this task. This result displayer can be extended to format the results of more specialized results in a more compact way. However, there is a danger that the callback display gets crowded very soon. It can only provide a rough overview. Therefore, all results arriving at the home application can be stored on disk for offline analysis with third-party tools.

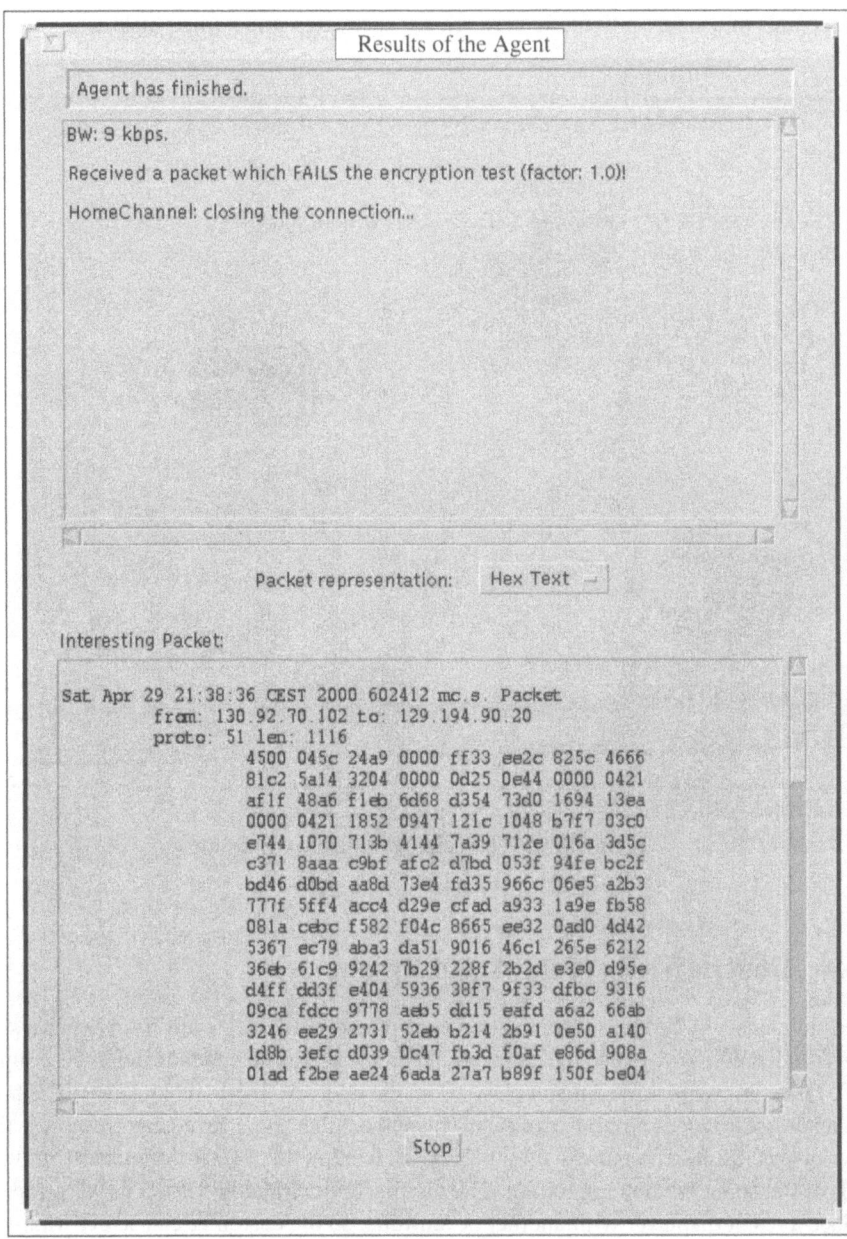

Figure 3.11: The agent result display window.

Figure 3.12 shows a node topology and measurement results as presented by the display.
Keep in mind that the display only shows the inter-provider connectivity. On the screen
the internals of a single provider's network are abstracted into a filled disk.

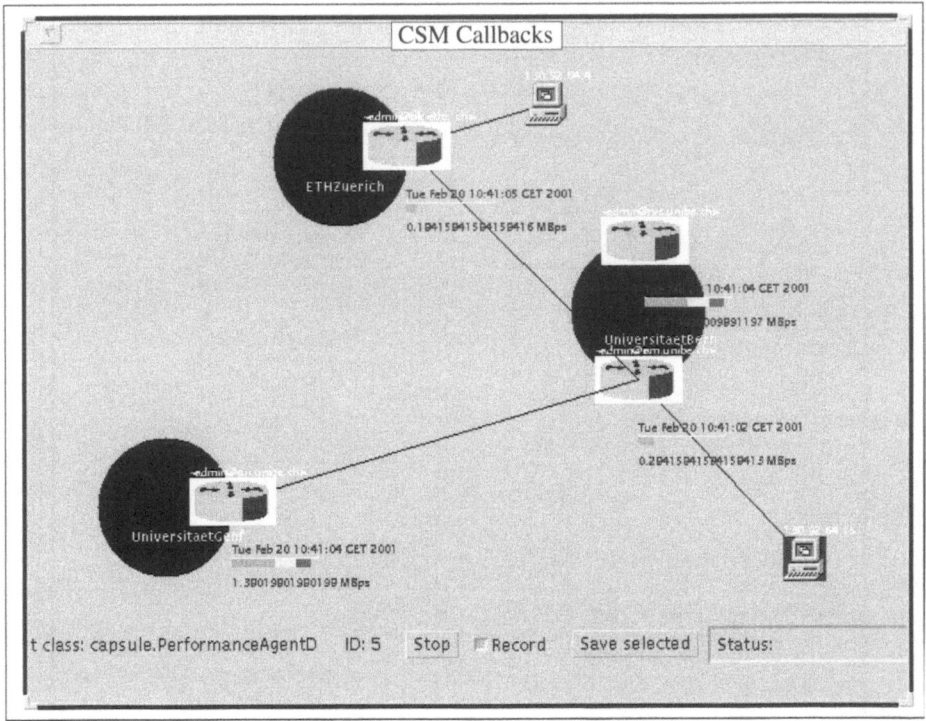

Figure 3.12: The callback display window.

3.6.4   Generic Views of the Agent Results

The implemented CSM home application provides several visualizations of agent results.
The visualization always use the same architectonic principle which is depicted in figure
3.13. There is a standardized result class (from the `clientserver` package). The home
application introduces a number of result displayers that use a Java canvas to draw their
view of the result. The canvas may be a GUI window or a GUI component provided
by Java's abstract windowing toolkit. The architectonic principle allows the developer to
replace a result displayer with another at run-time, so the customer can select what view
of the results (s)he wants. A developer can easily introduce new subclasses of results
that carry more information. (S)he can also write new displayers that can show the new
aspects of the results. Nevertheless, the old displayers will also still work because of the
inheritance mechanism.

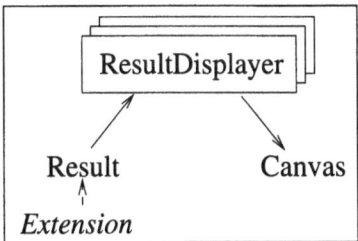

Figure 3.13: The visualization priciple.

The home application introduces several result displayers. One uses the character string representation supported by each result object. There is also a small collection of result displayers that display the IP packet that a result object can contain. It supports a text representation that also shows the packet's payload interpreted as ASCII characters. This is useful when monitoring an ASCII character based protocol such as http. Then, there is the traditional hexadecimal representation already shown in figure 3.11. As a special feature the home application introduces displayers that represent the packet payload as a matrix of colored boxes. This can be useful to analyze encryption and to detect patterns in the traffic. Figure 3.14 shows such a graphical representation of two packets. Each colored box represents a byte value of the payload. The packet to the right is encrypted. The encryption scrambles the patterns. All colors appear with a similar probability. The packet to the left is a BSP message [BGB01]. It is not designed to be human readable, but still it exposes some visible patterns. At the bottom of the packet there is a digital signature which becomes visible when displayed like that.

For agents that are forwarded and thus use the callback mechanism the CSM implementation introduces a new result class named `NumericResults` that can carry an array of floating point numbers along with an averaged number. The averaged number is then used by the value displayer to give an overview of the currently measured state (see figure 3.12). This simplifies the job for the home application, which may otherwise become a bottleneck if many agents use the callback mechanism at the same time. The agents can preprocess several results and aggregate them in a NumericResults object, thus disburden the home application. The new result class and the callback result displayer are another example of the presented architectonic principle and they show how new result types and suitable result displayers can be added to the home application implementation.

3.7 CSM Internetworking Support

Section 2.5.1 identified the need for an advanced support for large scale deployment of the CSM infrastructure. The infrastructure should provide a name space, node contacting information, and dynamic node topology information. Section 2.5.1 proposes to extend existing Internet protocols. For the proof-of-concept, however, a simpler implementation of the necessary mechanisms suffices. Here, each CSM node has two special configuration

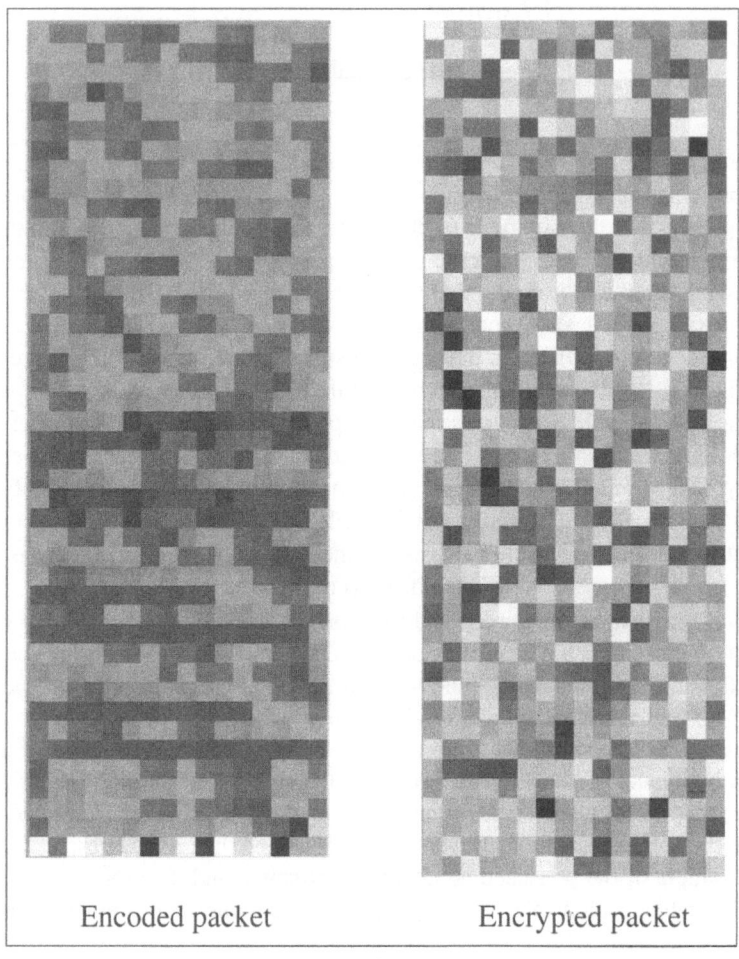

Encoded packet   Encrypted packet

Figure 3.14: Graphical representations of two packets.

files, one for providing name and contacting information and one for topology information. Note that nodes having access to the same file system can of course share these files. This approach is not scalable to large numbers of nodes. If there are several thousand nodes, then the overlay topology may become difficult to maintain. Yet, the CSM implementation is intended as a proof of concept. The CSM experiments did at no time have access to a number of monitoring points which is even near the critical size.

Nevertheless, the CSM nodes implement a dynamic routing protocol for maintaining an overlay topology so that agents can be routed from node to node. Keep also in mind that the interfaces between the node and the classes that provide the advanced support functionalities (that access the configuration files) are factored out in separate classes. Thus, if a solution based on existing Internet protocols will be implemented, it is easy to integrate it in the existing node implementation.

3.7.1 Name and Topology Information

All node identifiers are encoded in an e-mail-like naming style such as `admin@node1.-iam.unibe.ch`. This is compliant with a possible future integration of node name resolution with DNS lookups. E-mail addresses also work well with the PGP encryption and authentication infrastructure. In order to have a compact solution, CSM integrates the contact information of nodes with the contact information of customers. Table 3.4 shows how records of a name lookup file are structured. Each identifier is associated with an IP or DNS address where a node runs. The node listens for the CSM protocol on the given port number. The port number is not fixed so that several nodes may run on a single machine. For normal deployment of CSM there is no need to run several nodes on one machine. Yet, this feature was convenient for testing CSM nodes. The contacting information record also contains a field that names the owner organization of the node (the name of the provider). The contacting information file mixes nodes with customer identifiers. Therefore it also needs a flag that distinguishes them.

Table 3.4: The contacting information file structure.

Identifier	DNS address	IP	Port	Organization	Customer
admin@node1.cui.unige.ch		129.194.71.53	1998	Uni Geneva	false
admin@sniff.iam.unibe.ch	milou.unibe.ch		1998	Uni Berne	false
mguenter@iam.unibe.ch	balu.unibe.ch	130.92.64.15	0	RVS	true

The topology lookup table allows the nodes to determine their neighbor nodes. The nodes use this information to set up routing tables that allow them to forward agents from node to node in a similar way as IP packets are forwarded in the Internet. The customer can use the CSM protocol to query the nodes about neighboring information in order to learn about new nodes. Agents that use the callback mechanism can automatically transmit neighboring information to the home application. The home application is then able to reconstruct the part of the node topology that is interesting for the customer. The node also uses the topology lookup table to store fixed IP addresses of customers. Then these customers can forward agents in the hop-by-hop mode (see section 2.4) which allows the customer to monitor a complete route. Table 3.5 shows a sample of the structure of the topology lookup file. There, two nodes are neighbors of each other and one of them sits on an access router of a customer (mguenter@iam.unibe.ch - compare with table 3.4).

Table 3.5: The topology lookup file structure.

Identifier	List of neighbors
admin@node1.cui.unige.ch	admin@sniff.iam.unibe.ch
admin@sniff.iam.unibe.ch	admin@node1.cui.unige.ch:mguenter@iam.unibe.ch

For each node, the topology file contains a list of identifiers that declare who the node's neighbors are. Note that the nodes need the contacting information file to map node identifiers to network addresses. They also need a routing mechanism to learn more about the topology than just neighboring information.

3.7.2   Routing

At the startup of the node, the node consults the topology table to learn about its neighbors. It initializes a routing table and inserts the neighbor contacting information gained from the appropriate file. The CSM nodes implement a distance vector routing algorithm that uses the hop-count as distance metric. The routing protocol is thus similar to the RIP routing protocol of the early Internet. The routing records for the neighbor nodes thus include a hop-count value set to one. The routing mechanism of the node obtains routing records from two sources. As already mentioned, at the startup of the node the topology table provides the names of the immediate neighbor nodes and neighbor customers. Other routing record candidates are received from neighbor nodes through the CSM protocol. The routing mechanism uses these candidates and enters all those records of targets that are not yet in the routing table or replaces the records of targets that have a higher hop-count in the routing table. All updated records are bundled into one CSM message, their hop-count is incremented by one and the bundle is then broadcasted to the neighbor nodes.

Here is an excerpt from the class definition of routing records:

```
public class RoutingRecord implements java.io.Serializable {
    public int IP;          // Target.
    public String nextHop;  // A node identifier.
    public int hopCount=0;
...
}
```

3.8 Organization of the Source Code

The CSM Java source code is grouped into packages. This provides more modularity, safety and manageability to the implementation. The CSM implementation proposes two installations: one for the customer (the home application and individual agents) and the other for the provider (the nodes). Both installations have packages that are uniquely used by them, some that they both share, and some that are only stubs. The stub packages are necessary if one installation must know some basic classes of that package but not all of them. The best example is the `capsule` package that bundles the agents. For the node installation it suffices to know the `capsule.Agent` class. The individual agent class and its helper classes are dynamically uploaded by the CSM protocol when the customer sends the agents. Here is a complete list of the packages and their purpose:

- **application.** This package hosts stand alone Java applications that can be used in conjunction with CSM agents. An example application is a traffic generator.

- **capsule.** All CSM agents are implemented in this package.

- **clientserver.** The CSM protocol classes and helpers are implemented here.

- **config.** This package groups the classes that help the node or other applications read and parse configuration information from files.

- **filter.** All classes related to filtering are implemented in this package.

- **homeApplication.** The classes that implement the home application are bundled into this package.

- **netgui.** This package hosts the classes that help to display a network topology and callback agent results.

- **node.** This package bundles most of the classes relevant for the node implementation.

- **topology.** Here are the classes that implement the node routing.

- **utils.** This package contains helper classes that are useful in other contexts, too, such as the PGPEncoder class that provides access to PGP encryption and authentication.

Table 3.6 shows how the installations use the packages:

Table 3.6: The use of the packages by the two installation variants.

Package	Provider installation	Customer installation
application	not used	exclusively used
capsule	stub	used
clientserver	shared	shared
config	exclusively used	not used
filter	shared	shared
homeApplication	not used	exclusively used
netgui	not used	exclusively used
node	used	stub
topology	used	stub
utils	shared	shared

Chapter 4

Applications of Service Monitoring Agents

Chapter 2 showed that the successful market introduction of new IP services will be coupled with the introduction of a customer-based service monitoring infrastructure. This chapter will give examples of new IP services and of CSM agents capable of monitoring them. Neither the list of services nor the collection of agents discussed here are complete, but CSM is generic and can thus easily be extended. For each new service a new monitoring agent can be implemented (or an old one may be adapted). This can be performed by customers, providers, or a third-party vendor. This chapter focuses on the IP services discussed in the introduction of this book: a virtual private network service and differentiated services for the Internet.

4.1   Monitoring a Virtual Private Network Service

Virtual Private Networks (VPN) for the Internet [FH98a, FH98b] provide a transparent and secure mechanism to interconnect remote sites with IP (see figure 1.2). IP packets are encapsulated in new IP packets when entering the Internet (tunneling). The payload of the new packet (the original packet) is encrypted. The original IP addresses may be private (not routed in the public Internet) [RMK+96], so they do not have to be world-wide unique. Thus, VPNs allow the customer to use an arbitrary number of unregistered addresses in their Intranet[1]. Virtual private networks over the Internet are a cheap and secure alternative to leased line based private corporate networks. They take advantage of the ubiquitousness of the Internet and the trend towards Intranets. The Internet Engineering Task Force (IETF) proposed the VPN standard IPSec [KA98c], which is supported by many vendors nowadays. However, VPNs and especially their cryptographic mechanisms are difficult to understand and manage [GBK99]. Therefore, service providers begin to of-

---

[1]Intranets: Corporate networks based on IP technology.

fer VPN services where they setup and manage the tunnel endpoints for their customers. However, the security is transparent to the customer. The customer believes that all the IP traffic leaving the network is encrypted. But encryption is computational intensive. How can the customer be sure that the provider is really performing the IPSec protocol properly and is not just, for instance, compressing the payload? This question is not a purely academic one. In the year 2000 the question arose in two different IPSec related e-mail discussion forums [Fre00, Sec00]. There are different reasons why people need the ability to monitor a VPN service. For example, the customer's technical personnel may have to give an account of the expenses for a VPN service to the higher management of a corporation. They therefore need a way to demonstrate the security that would be gained by means of the service in question. The customers also need a method to examine the VPN service in order to make an informed decision whether the service is of any interest to them. The customer may also have to integrate a VPN service into a corporate-wide security policy which may, for example, specify that the private address structure of the corporate Intranet will be hidden and that all IP traffic traveling over public infrastructure is encrypted. Usually such business policies require processes that guarantee or enforce policy-conformance. The discussion on the expert mail lists concluded that there are two powerful ways to check conformance of IPSec VPNs. On the one hand the traditional method consists of interoperability tests: if products of several vendors cooperate in a given mode, then that mode must have been implemented properly. However, most VPNs use only equipment of a single supplier in order to ease the management. Furthermore, if a service provider operates the VPN service, the customer will probably neither be able nor allowed to perform interoperability tests on the provider's equipment. The second approach for validating a VPN service is introspection into the service traffic: mail list authors suggest `tcpdump` for this purpose but of course this is not an option for out-sourced VPNs with regard to security issues. Here, the proposed customer-based service monitoring infrastructure comes to play. It provides a safe way to service inspection.

4.1.1 Functionality of a VPN Control Agent

Given an agent infrastructure as described in section 2, we have many possibilities to check whether the VPN provider implements the service as promised using specialized agents. Such a VPN monitoring agent requests (some of) the packets from the node that are exchanged between the tunnel endpoints and that belong to IPSec traffic (protocol 51 Authentication Header (AH) or 50 Encapsulating Security Payload (ESP) - see section 1.2.2). The nodes of VPN providers can accept requests for monitoring ESP traffic, because the ESP payload should be encrypted, so the privacy of the sender is not compromised. For AH, the provider may enforce that only the header bytes are delivered. Paranoid providers may also limit such access to agents owned by customers that subscribe to their VPN service. The agent can thus monitor the IPSec traffic. Here are some specific checks that can be carried out by CSM agents:

- The customer can occasionally send out agents to the egress peering points of the access network (see figure 2.1). These agents will run outside of the customer's private network and can monitor all traffic that enters from and leaves for the public Internet. The agents check for traffic that use internal network addresses of the customer's network in their header. The agents should not find any such packets because these addresses ought to be private. If the service is working properly, the privately addressed packets are encapsulated in the payload of a packet with the public tunnel-endpoint addresses.

- The customer can send out agents that monitor the IPSec protocol activities. Agents can, for example, monitor the presence[2] of the key exchange protocol IKE (UDP to port 500).

- The agents can also analyze the packet structure to verify if the proper tunneling modes are used. It can examine the IP protocol field (50 for ESP, 51 for AH) and possibly the next header field(s).

- The agents can analyze the protocol fields of the IPSec headers. For example, it can use the sequence number to learn about lost packets. It can use the security parameters index to identify different tunnels.

- A VPN agent can collect statistics about the fragmentation of IPSec packets. IPSec adds additional header and eventually trailer bytes to the IP packets. This can cause packets to exceed a local MTU value and thus lead to packet fragmentation. Problem reports on the VPN mail list indicate that fragmentation is a major cause of IP-VPNs problems ranging from performance degradation to service outage [Bir].

- VPN monitoring agents can collect data at several points in the network. Thus an agent may monitor the traffic inside of the customer's private network (plaintext) and correlate that with data collected in the provider network (IPSec). Using this approach the customer can, for example, detect if a provider uses the same tunnel for several customers.

- The customer can test the authentication mechanism of the provider. The customer lets an agent fetch an IPSec packet in the provider network. Another agent checks for a duplicated packet at the far end of the VPN tunnel. The customer retransmits that copied packet thus launching a replay-attack. IPSec should detect the attack and discard the packet. The agent can also carry out other traditional performance monitoring tasks, such as recording throughput and jitter of a VPN tunnel.

- IPSec agents can be used to correlate arrival times of a given packet in order to learn e.g. the one-way delay of the transmission and the time for encryption and decryption of a packet.

- The customer can use statistical tests to validate the encryption and authentication algorithms used by IPSec.

---

[2]The IKE protocol of IPSec is encrypted, therefore not much more than the presence can be monitored.

4.1.2   Statistical Tests on Cryptographic Algorithms

The VPN monitoring agent has (albeit limited) possibilities to validate the quality of the encryption as well as of the authentication algorithms used for the protection of the VPN. The output of cryptographic algorithms hides the structure of the input. Value accumulations and correlations within the input data values are washed away. The output bits look as if created by a uniformly distributed and independent source of random zeroes and ones. If a cryptographic algorithm exposes regularities, these can be used to break it. In the area of random number generators there are many statistical tests that reveal statistical irregularities. These tests can therefore be used to detect a weakness in an encryption scheme. Note that the reverse implication is not necessarily true: even if an encryption scheme is useful as a random number generator, it may still be insecure. The use of statistical tests to find weaknesses in an encryption scheme is widely accepted. For example, the National Institute for Standardization (NIST) used a suite of statistical tests in the evaluation process for the Advanced Encryption Standard (AES) [Sot00]. One of the AES candidate algorithms will replace the ubiquitous but timeworn DES encryption algorithm. Note that several[3] candidate algorithms did not pass the statistical tests and were consequently rejected.

A statistical test suite.   We implemented a statistical test suite with the programming language Java. The framework (see figure 4.1) is modular so that the input data can come from different sources and that different tests can be used. The raw data is encapsulated in singletons which format the data into numeric values or raw bytes (samples). Each *singletons* object represents a stream of sample values. The source of the samples may, for example, be files or user input or live encryption algorithms. The singletons thus hide the details of the source of the data. The accumulator classifies the samples delivered by the singletons' object. For example, it may count byte values (256 classes) or count the number of samples that have a higher value than a threshold (two classes). The accumulator also contains a distribution which defines the probability for each value class that the accumulator uses. The test compares the accumulated occurrences in the value classes with the distribution. It calculates the probability that the sample values really reflect the expected probability. Of course, the expected probabilities (the distribution) depend on the classification used by the accumulator. The test applies the hypothesis that the encrypted traffic has the same statistical properties as a uniformly distributed and independent bit stream. This leads to an expected distribution. Then the test calculates the probability that the hypothesis is true given a concrete distribution of samples. If the test result is very improbable, then the encryption algorithm is probably not safe. Note that the test output can be used as singletons again since the test provides a probability of the following form: chances that a the hypothesis is true are within 98 percent. We can then test several sets of samples and classify them into two categories: the ones within the 98 percent and the ones that are not. We know the expected distribution (0.98 for 'in' and 0.02 for 'out'). Thus we can now calculate the probability of the hypothesis using a whole series of tests.

---

[3]4 out of 15.

The next paragraph shows how tests can evaluate the output of an accumulator. Most of that material originates from [Knu81] and is described in more detail there.

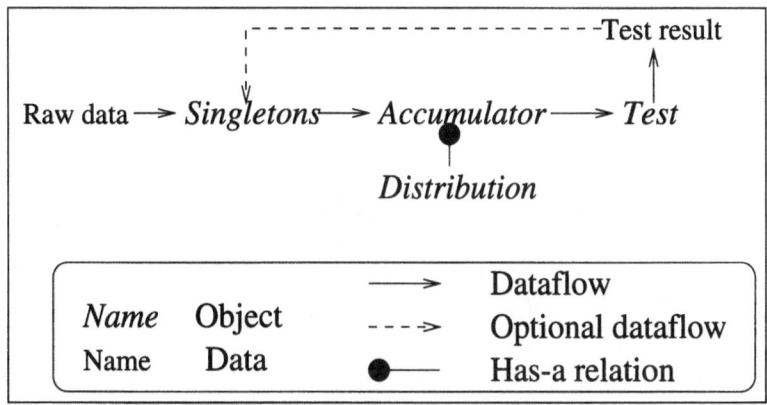

Figure 4.1: Statistical test framework.

An example of a statistical test: the byte frequency test. Here is an instance of the framework that is both illustrating and useful. The byte frequency test verifies if the bytes in a bit stream are equally distributed. It interprets the input as raw bytes. The accumulator counts the occurrence of each byte value; it thus classifies the raw data into 256 categories. Keep in mind that such an accumulation is also called a histogram. When a significant amount of bytes is counted (this depends on the test), then the test analyzes how the bytes are distributed in the value space. Encrypted data should be uniformly distributed, so each byte value should occur about the same number of times. However, if every byte value would occur exactly the same number of times, this would be suspicious, too. Figure 4.2 shows an example histogram together with the expected distribution.

The byte frequency test uses the well-known χ^2 statistics [Knu81] to quantify the conformity of the classified values with the distribution (to evaluate the test). Assume we have k categories and Y_s samples fall into category s. Let n be the number of samples and p_s the probability that a sample falls into category s. Then the χ^2 statistics V is defined as:

$$V = \sum_{1 \leq s \leq k} \frac{(Y_s - np_s)^2}{np_s} \tag{4.1}$$

For each category the square of the deviation between the counted samples Y_s and the expected number of samples np_s is calculated. This deviation is put in relation to the number of expected samples and summed up over all categories. For the byte-frequency test each byte value has the same probability, thus ($p_s = 1/256$) holds for all s. The nice thing about the χ^2 statistics is that it provides a single value V that can be directly mapped to a probability. The explicit formula is rather complex. In order to determine the

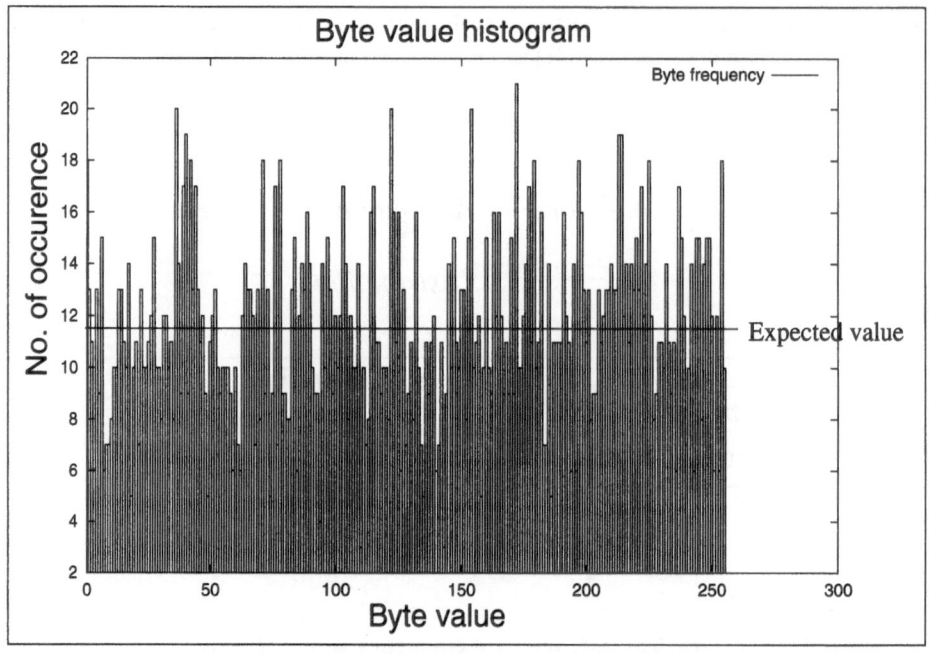

Figure 4.2: The histogram of byte values.

probability of the calculated V value, there are tables that map V values to probabilities [Knu81]. This mapping depends on the degree of freedom of the category classification. The degree of freedom is the number of categories minus one $(k - 1)$. For the byte frequency test the degree of freedom is thus 255. The table provides information of the form as follows: with a probability of 99 percent V should be less than 331.5. If not, the deviations between the number of occurrences and the expectations from the distribution is too large. For the byte frequency test the χ^2 distribution table also indicates that with a probability of 99 percent V should be larger than 205.5. If not, the number of occurrences in each category is *too close* to the expected value. Note that the χ^2 probability table can only be applied if a significant number of samples has been collected. The number of samples should be big enough so that the expected number for each category (np_s) is at least five. So for the byte frequency test $(n\frac{1}{256} \geq 5)$, thus at least $n = 1280$ bytes should be considered. The test for the byte distribution depicted in figure 4.2 delivers $V = 274.9$, and for this reason the data source passes the test.

The run test. The run test is a powerful statistical test that is sensitive to correlations in consecutive data values. Instead of classifying the encrypted data by the byte values, the run test works on floating point numbers. For example, four raw data bytes are interpreted as one floating point number. The numbers are then divided in sequences of monotonically increasing numbers.

For instance, the sequence $(-33.2, 104.4, -45.8, 3.0, 34.7, 7.1, -19.3, -93.2, 1.1)$ is interpreted as five sequences: $(-33.2, 104.4, |-45.8, 3.0, 34.7, |7.1, |-19.3, |-93.2, 1.1)$. Then the sequences are categorized according to their length. Usually, there are 6 classes: sequences of the length 1, 2, 3, 4, 5, and 6 or more. The expected distribution of these sequence lengths is not trivial, because the length of a sequence depends on the length of the previous one. Therefore, the run test needs a fairly complex calculation of a statistics V in order to be conform with the χ^2 distribution table. However, with a simple trick the calculation becomes much easier. You simply omit the sample right after the end of a sequence. Then the sequences lengths are independent and the χ^2 distribution table can be used directly. When this trick is applied, the probability $P(r)$ for a sequence of length r is:

$$P(r) = \frac{1}{(r-1)!(r+1)} \tag{4.2}$$

Table 4.1 shows the expected distribution of the 6 categories of the run test.

Table 4.1: Run test distribution.

Sequence length	Probability
1	1/2
2	1/3
3	1/8
4	1/30
5	1/144
6 and more	1/720

Online calculation of V. Using formula 4.1 the agents have to iterate through all categories each time they want to evaluate a test. If they perform the test too frequently, their performance may suffer (especially for the byte frequency test where there are 256 categories). However, if they perform the tests too infrequently, then a statistical irregularity may be washed away by the following data. Therefore, we transformed the calculation formula so that for each additional value in category s, V can be calculated directly with constant computational complexity. Let V_n be the statistic calculated for the n-th sample value. Then:

$$V_{n+1} = \frac{n(V_n + n) + \frac{2Y_s + 1}{p_s}}{n+1} - n - 1 \tag{4.3}$$

With this formula both the byte-frequency and the run-test can be executed fine-grained and online.

Evaluation. Both the byte-frequency test and the run test use the χ^2 distribution table to evaluate the test results. The byte-frequency test checks if the data values are equally distributed and the run-test verifies if there are correlations in the data values. So both tests complement each other but at the same time can share code. Therefore, the implemented VPN monitoring agent uses these two tests as encryption verification tests. Note that there are countless other statistical tests [Knu81, Sot00]. CSM allows the customers to use the tests of their choice. The two proposed statistical tests can disclose providers who use a weak encryption scheme or who just compress the payload instead of encrypting it. Keep in mind that IPSec is modular. IPSec can indeed use arbitrary cryptographic algorithms for the encryption and authentication. It can even use the so-called null transformation that leaves the input unchanged. In [BGKL00] we performed the presented tests (plus the Anderson-Darling test proposed in [PAMM98]) on 2 Megabytes of encrypted IPSec ESP payload and on a compressed archive of the same size. All tests were able to single out the compressed file as not being encrypted. An advantage of statistical tests is that they are generic. Compare it to alternatives, e.g. an agent that scans for English words in the payload. While this may be faster and easier to implement, even a simplistic and completely insecure algorithm, such as ROT13, could be used to circumvent the agent. In contrast to that, the statistical properties, which the presented tests aim at, are an intrinsic property that every well encrypted traffic must posses. Therefore, the statistical tests cannot only be applied to reveal that a provider tries to avoid the encryption work but it can also be used to detect implementation problems, such as the Linux IPSec implementation problem mentioned in [Den00]. Denker points out that, under certain circumstances, traffic from the private network may leak out unencrypted into the public network when the machine hosting the tunnel endpoint is restarted. Furthermore, the statistical tests can reveal if a provider uses an encryption scheme in the weak electronic code book (ECB) mode. The ECB mode does not include the previous block's encryption into the encryption of the current data block. Thus, two equal plaintext blocks result in two equal ciphertext blocks. Equal plaintext blocks (e.g. all bits set to zero) in a data stream are not uncommon. A duplicated packet of 1400 bytes size will cause the statistical tests to indicate a problem.

Nevertheless, there is also a limit to what the statistical tests can detect. First, and foremost: even if the traffic passes the encryption test, it may still be encrypted with a weak algorithm. If you use, for example, the Java random number generator as input for a stream cipher, then the resulting traffic will pass the tests [BGKL00]. However, this random number generator is based on a linear congruential generator. These generators are easily broken [Sch96]. Also, the performed tests were not able to distinguish between encryption algorithms that use different key lengths. A 40-bit DES encryption passed the tests as well as a 112-bit 3DES encryption did. In theory [GBB00], when testing a data amount in the same order of magnitude as the key space, the statistical tests could reveal the difference. To prove that hypothesis, one would have to compare at least two times 2^{40} encrypted blocks (8 byte). These are 16 Tera bytes of data and thus beyond our hardware capacity. Nevertheless, somebody may think of more intelligent tests that are, for instance, tailored to an algorithm and that try to perform a cryptanalysis against it. With CSM agents the test can then easily be used by the customers.

It is important to note that traditional stationary control programs located at customer premises are not able to perform the VPN checks described in this section. They have no insight in the service as it is delivered in the provider networks. In addition to this, the functionality of the VPN agents is too complex to be implemented in traditional network monitoring applications that collect information with SNMP [CFSD90] or in web-based network management entries.

Implementation. We implemented a virtual private network monitoring agent for the customer-based service monitoring platform described in chapter 3. The agent can perform either one of the two presented statistical tests to ensure that VPN traffic is encrypted and authenticated. The agent also verifies that the IPSec protocols are used in the proper modes by analyzing the packet headers. In the test layout this was AH in tunnel mode encapsulating ESP in transport mode. Moreover, the agent observes the throughput and packet loss of the monitored tunnel. The agent reports the measured tunnel throughput to its home application on a regular basis. It also reports special events, such as packet loss, a malformed IPSec transformation or a failed encryption/authentication test. In the last case it sends back the monitored packet that caused the test to fail so that a human operator can verify the finding. Figure 3.11 showed the reports that were sent by a VPN agent that was able to demonstrate its ability to detect unencrypted traffic on a *real* VPN tunnel. For that purpose we used our VPN management tool [KBG00] to hot-swap a properly encrypted VPN tunnel with one that does authentication only. The VPN agent immediately detects and reports this. However, performance tests indicated some limitations, since the statistical tests require computational power (much less than encryption, though). Running on a Sparc ULTRA 5 with a 269 MHz CPU, the agent could test 1.5 Mbps encrypted data with the run-test and 1 Mbps data with the byte-frequency test (for more details see chapter 5). Note that in case the agent wants to monitor a line with higher throughput, it can choose not to analyze every byte in every packet, since sample testing will also suffice to detect a VPN service misconfiguration.

4.2   Service Level Agreement Monitoring

Traditional service level agreements for Internet services are contracts that describe the business relationship between a customer and an Internet service provider (ISP). The SLA describes the nature of the service provided, its price, and clauses for special cases, e.g. what happens when one of the agreement partners violates the agreement [Ver99]. A traditional IP service provides Internet connectivity. The service is relatively simple but still the ISPs try to differentiate their offerings, e.g. by bundling the IP service with additional services (help-desk, web hosting, e-mail hosting, etc.). We will not discuss the add-on services in this section. Instead, let us focus on the pure IP service and its possible differentiations in SLAs. Even for pure connectivity there are performance metrics that are used in todays SLAs:

- **Reliability.** The reliability of the IP service is usually measured in the uptime of the network. The provider may also ensure upper bounds for connectivity outage times or outage counts. The provider may also guarantee to solve network problems within a given time (outage resolution time). The connectivity can also be partially damaged. Reliability metrics may thus also include limits on packet loss rates and on error rates.

- **Responsiveness.** A provider may guarantee an upper bound of the IP round-trip time for certain destinations. Today, such guarantees exist but are limited to the network of the ISP. Responsiveness guarantees can also include statements about one-way delays and response times of applications (e.g. web servers).

The SLA normally also defines how the performance is measured, thus it describes the SLA monitoring. Given today's infrastructure it is the provider who measures the SLA conformance. The provider then delivers reports on a regular basis (typically each month). The customers are left with no other choice than to trust the report of the provider. Moreover, the long reporting interval averages away the impact of network problems. For example, a 99 percent uptime guarantee may look good on the SLA paper. A seven-hour connectivity outage can however cost a fortune to e-commerce companies, but it is still SLA conformable if it occurs only once a month.

The proposed customer-based service monitoring infrastructure allows the customers to test conformance to the SLA metrics themselves. In the case of measuring network outages the mobile agents of CSM are particularly useful. Applications that sit in the customer network are by definition cut off during the outage while roaming agents reside in the Internet and can study the problem further.

With the introduction of quality-of-service (QoS) mechanisms in the Internet the provider can differentiate their Internet service offerings even more. They can offer new and more distinct guarantees defined on more fine-grained performance metrics. Note that all metrics of the pure connectivity service can be applied to a QoS enhanced Internet service. Thus, simpler variants of the QoS monitoring agents can also be used for plain IP monitoring. The guarantees that a provider offers can be quantitative (e.g. in bits per second) or qualitative (e.g. low latency). They can be absolute or relative to other service classes. Here is a list of traffic properties that may be involved in the guarantees. Different properties may be assigned to different classes of traffic, making the range of SLA diversification even vaster.

- Traffic loss (e.g. in bytes per byte).

- Erroneous packets (e.g. in packets per byte).

- Throughput (e.g. in bytes per second).

- Goodput. The goodput is the throughput of application data and thus application specific.

- One-way delay and round-trip delay (e.g. in milliseconds).

- Jitter (e.g. in milliseconds).

This diversity of metrics is a strong argument for the author's CSM infrastructure. CSM is generic enough to allow the customer to monitor all presented kinds of service level specifications. Therefore we will study CSM agents for QoS services in more detail.

4.3 Agents for Measuring QoS Parameters

This section presents quality-of-service measuring strategies using mobile CSM agents, some agents that implement the strategies, and selected results that these agents delivered in test scenarios. It follows a classification of the measurement approaches. The simplest approach is sending a single measurement agent that carries out a measurement and returns the result(s). These are *passive* and *stand-alone* measurements. If the customer sends out several agents and compares their results, this is a *distributed measurement*. If the customer uses additional applications to generate traffic and the agents use that traffic to derive results, then an *active measurement* is carried out. Some distributed measurement agents may need *synchronized* clocks. The agents will hardly be able to synchronize themselves. However, the nodes of some providers may use synchronized clocks. Their clocks may be synchronized with the Network Time Protocol (NTP) [Mil92] or with a satellite-based system, such as the Global Positioning System (GPS). Then, the packet timestamps that the agents use (see section 2.3.2) refer to synchronized clocks, so the measurements of these agents are synchronous. If the measurement agent uses knowledge about higher-level protocols (e.g. if it knows how to collect TCP sequence numbers or how an IPSec header is structured), then the agent is referred to as *protocol dependent*. Note that measurements relying on synchronized clocks are by definition distributed (else, the synchronization does not make sense). The following sections describe CSM-based measurements on the traffic properties listed in the previous section.

4.3.1 Throughput Measurements

IP throughput measurements can be performed by simple stand-alone CSM agents. The customer sends an agent of this kind to the desired location in the provider network. The agent is equipped with a filter that specifies what traffic flows should be measured. The customer can select to monitor everything ranging from subnet-to-subnet traffic to specific micro-flows. We implemented an agent that counts the transported bytes during a configurable interval and reports the throughput after every interval. The agent uses the `length` field of the IP packet to count bytes, so the agent applies a filter that requests only the IP headers from the node. The agent is thus very light in weight and fast. The simple version of the IP throughput measuring agent can be improved by adding protocol knowledge. Then the agent can analyze the IP packets and extract the payload of higher layer protocols. The agent can, for example, subtract the bytes of IPSec headers and trailers in order to calculate the pure tunnel throughput. Furthermore, the agent can be used for distributed measurements. In general, the customer will have more information about the service state at his/her disposal when (s)he knows about the state at several locations in the network. A distributed measurement application of the simple throughput agent could be to learn about the routing of the providers. The customer sends out the agents to peering points in order to learn how much and what kind of his/her traffic passes there. The throughput agent can also measure the best-effort- to priority traffic ratio (e.g. for DiffServ).

Bottleneck Bandwidth Measurement.   Bottleneck bandwidth is a fundamental property of a network connection [Pax97]. The bottleneck bandwidth is the upper limit of how quickly the network can deliver a sender's data to a receiver. Usually the bottleneck bandwidth is the bandwidth of the slowest link on the path. Bottleneck bandwidth is relatively easy to measure. You need a sender who sends two packets immediately after each other (also called the *packet pair* estimation). The second packet must queue behind the first until the first is completely transmitted. The delay between the two packets therefore indicates the transmission time of the first packet. Ideally, the packets travel through an uncongested network. The packets then only become further apart if the next link is slower than the slowest previous one. So the delay between the two packets indicates the bandwidth of the slowest link on the path (the bottleneck). The bottleneck bandwidth δ is thus $\delta = b_A/(t_B - t_A)$ where b_A is the size of the first packet (A) in bytes and t_A and t_B are the arrival times of the packet. One very convenient property of the bottleneck bandwidth test is that it does not require synchronized clocks. The receiver only has to compare the arrival times of two (or more) packets.

Usually the bottleneck bandwidth is determined through active measurements. A sending application sends a number of packets in a short sequence and a receiving application determines δ value before it considers that this value is a maximum candidate. We implemented a *passive bottleneck measurement agent*. It calculates δ for each packet pair and selects the maximum. However, due to queuing effects caused by other traffic some δ values may be too small. The passive bottleneck agent levels this out in that a configurable number of consecutive packets must deliver the same δ. This will also prevent the problem of multi-link connections, such as ISDN, that cause wrong results with the packet pair method [Pax97]. Note that in the Internet the bottleneck bandwidth is not always constant. For example, route changes may influence it. The implemented agent is able to cope with this by using a soft-state mechanism for the current δ. Thus, after a configurable time, the δ is reset to an initial state and the measurement restarts. Figure 4.3 shows the results delivered by a passive bottleneck bandwidth measurement agent (in *micro*seconds - μs[4].) . The agent monitors traffic on a PC that is connected to a 10 Mbit Ethernet. It filters traffic coming from a neighbor 100 Mbit Ethernet. After about 12 seconds the agent found a bottleneck bandwidth of 1.22 MBytes which is very close to the theoretical maximum of 10 Mbits. Figure 4.3 also depicts how from time to time the agent confirms the bottleneck bandwidth. Keep in mind that the monitoring node was not in a productive network. Therefore, the test setting included artificially generated UDP background traffic. The passive bottleneck bandwidth agent will detect the bottleneck bandwidth only if an application rapidly sends packets at least in a short period of time. An FTP session transferring a file of about 100 KByte will do.

---

[4]$1s = 10^6 \mu s$

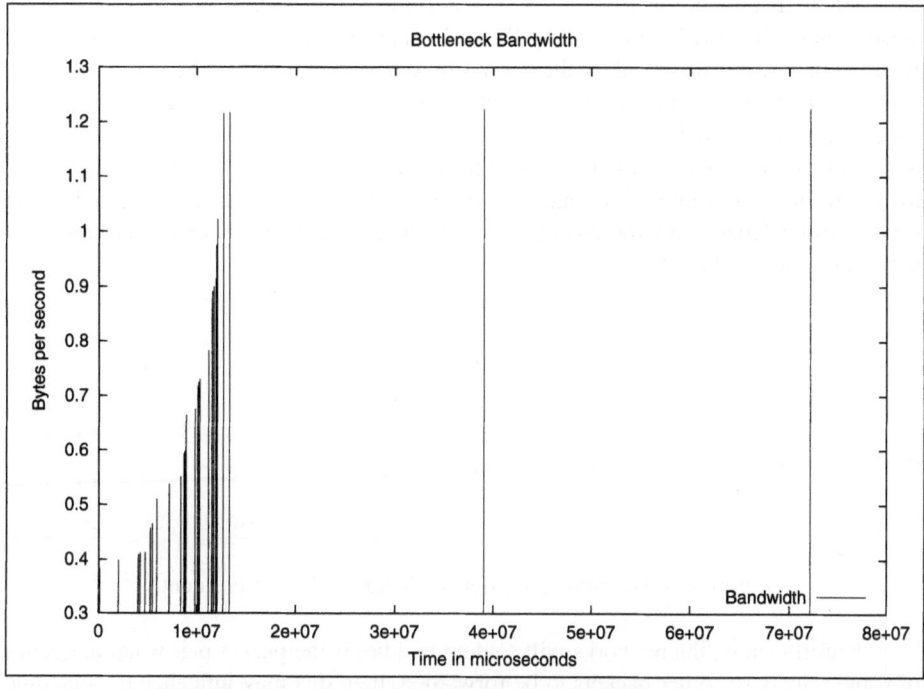

Figure 4.3: Real network bottleneck bandwidth measurement.

With the CSM infrastructure the traditional sender-receiver based bottleneck band-width measurement can be extended. Several intermediate agents can all measure the δ value and thus play the role of the receiver. The customer can compare the results of these agents and learn about the *location* of the bottleneck link and about local congestion. For that purpose the agents measure the delay between two (or more) selected packets and send the results to the customer application for comparison. Figure 4.4 shows a dis-tributed measurement scenario with three provider networks (A-C) and three CSM nodes (M1-M3) on which bottleneck bandwidth agents execute. Here, the sender sends a packet pair and the agents measure the delay between the packets. First let us study the ideal case where the networks are idle. The agent at M1 can measure the delay and directly calculate the available bandwidth of provider A. The agent at M2 measures the same delay. This means that the bandwidth provided by B is at least as large as the bandwidth provided by A. If the bandwidth was smaller, the delay would have been larger. The bandwidth of B could still be larger than the bottleneck but since B received the packet pair already with the given delay, the delay does not become smaller. The agent at M3 measures a larger delay. It can now calculate the bandwidth provided by C. It is the bottleneck bandwidth for the whole connection. Note that with bidirectional traffic measurements and traffic sources using other paths the customer can eventually learn more about the unknown bottleneck bandwidth at B.

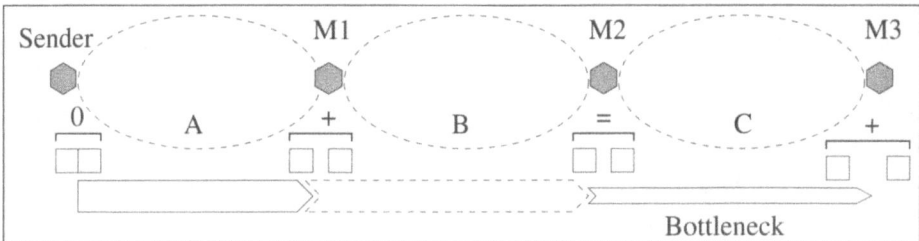

Figure 4.4: Distributed bottleneck bandwidth measurement.

Unfortunately, the networks will seldom be idle. If the packet pair waits in queues of some routers for other packets to be forwarded, then this may influence the outcome of the measurement. There are two cases where queuing has an influence on the mea-surements. (1) If a packet of a different source interleaves between the packet pair, then the delay between the packet increases and indicates a wrong bottleneck bandwidth. To avoid this, we can exploit the fact that the bottleneck bandwidth measurement provides an upper bound that is relatively constant. Therefore, the customer can carry out several mea-surements and compare the results. If there is an accumulation of a concrete bandwidth value, then this value is probably the true bottleneck bandwidth. (2) The other queuing influence is when foreign traffic causes the packet pair to queue before a fast link. Then, once the packets are forwarded the delay between them actually decreases. While this is bad for the simple end-to-end bottleneck bandwidth measurement, it is actually good for CSM-based distributed measurements. CSM can make use of the fact that this is the only case where the delay can actually decrease. Thus, if the delay between two packets has decreased from M1 to M2, then M1 can be regarded as the sending application that sends the two packets with no delay. The measured delay then allows the customer to deduce the bandwidth provided by B.

The tests showed that by comparing the delay between consecutive packets at different daytimes the customer can use CSM agents to collect an accurate picture of where congested links and bottleneck links are located. It is, however, important that the customer compares at different measuring points the inter-packet delays belonging to the *same* packets. Therefore, the distributed agents must possess a mechanism to identify packets as explained in the next section.

4.3.2   Coordination of Distributed Measurements

For security reasons the agent cannot read from network connections unless there is a node service for that purpose. Therefore, the home application cannot send control messages to the agent, and owing to this, the home application cannot directly synchronize the agent activities. If the node provides a synchronized clock service, then the customer can program the agents to synchronize their activities with this clock. There is another option to synchronize distributed measurement agents: the monitored traffic. The agents can inspect the monitored packet and see if they are relevant to them. If all agents of a distributed measurement setting use the same criterion, then their measurement is synchronized[5]. If the agents have protocol knowledge about protocols that synchronize their sender and receiver, then the agents can exploit this (implicit synchronization). Both protocols that built-up connections (e.g. TCP) and that use sequence numbers (e.g. ICMP) provide information that the agents can use to synchronize their measurements. Another possibility is that they synchronize on monitored packets that match a given hash value (explicit synchronization).

The Hash Agents.   We introduced a hash agent that hashes IP packets and compares them to a set of hash results. If there is a match, the hash agent can react in different ways. Thus, the customer can send IP packets that trigger agent activity once the agent sees such a packet. The customer can use this mechanism to coordinate distributed measurements. If the customer wants to compare test results of agents that perform sample tests, it may be important that they all use the same sample. The hash function can guarantee that (with an arbitrary high probability) the same packet is studied. The previously discussed bottleneck bandwidth agent is a good example. The sender of the packet pair uses packets with a random payload. It also calculates the hash of the packet's payload. The measurement agents know the hash result that they have to look for. Thus, they can easily identify the packets to be measured. The hash agent hashes from a configurable starting point in the IP packet up to an ending point. So, for example, the first 40 bytes of the UDP payload can be hashed. The customer can also configure the agent to match how many bits of the

---

[5]This does not mean that their clocks are synchronized, but that they perform the metrics on the same samples.

hash code must match. If, for example, the agent must only match 6 bits, then about every 64th packet matches.

The hash function call of the hash agent is generic; it can be replaced by an arbitrary hash function. CSM uses the IP checksum function [BBP88] and the Message Digest 5 (MD5) algorithm [Riv92] as hash functions. While the former is fast, the latter is secure. Using a secure hash function is interesting for agent security (see section 4.4), because even when an attacker knows what hash value the agent is waiting for, it is practically impossible to generate a packet with that hash and thus, for instance, to remotely manipulate the agent.

The Trigger Agent.   The trigger agent is a subtype of the hash agent and demonstrates one way to use the hash agents. Such an application generates a packet and its hash value in advance. The agent is fed with the hash value before it is sent out. Later, the application can send the generated packet to trigger the activity of the agent. The trigger agent encapsulates an arbitrary agent of the customer. It monitors the traffic only looking for a packet that matches a hash. From the moment this packet is received, the trigger agent delegates each packet or service result to the encapsulated agent. The trigger agent thus allows the customer to send an arbitrary agent and start it later by sending a special (possibly secret) start code. The trigger agent offers a generic way to add this functionality, e.g. to third-party agents.

The Trigger Application.   The customer also needs a way to send packets that trigger activities of hash agents. We implemented a so-called trigger application for demonstration purposes (see figure 4.5). The application can send a configurable number of UDP packets. The user has to specify the destination and the port number of the packets as well as the packet size and the number of times the packet should be sent. There are two buttons to press. The *create* button causes the application to create a packet with a random payload. It also establishes an MD5 hash of the created packet and displays it on the GUI. The hash is formatted like a static Java array declaration, so the user can cut-and-paste the hash into his/her measurement agent code. The user must then send out the agents. Finally, the user presses the *send* button for the packets to be sent. The trigger application serves as traffic generator for the distributed bottleneck bandwidth measurements described earlier.

4.3.3   One-Way Delay Measurements

One-way delay measurements require a synchronized clock. As mentioned before this can, for example, be provided by the node as a service to the agent. We implemented a one-way delay measuring agent suitable for distributed measurements. The agent is a sub-type of the hash agent. It records the arrival time for packets that match a hash. The hashing can be configured so that the agent performs sample tests on the background traffic, or it can be used to match only a particular packet generated by a customer application. The agent assumes the presence of synchronized clocks. Since implementing

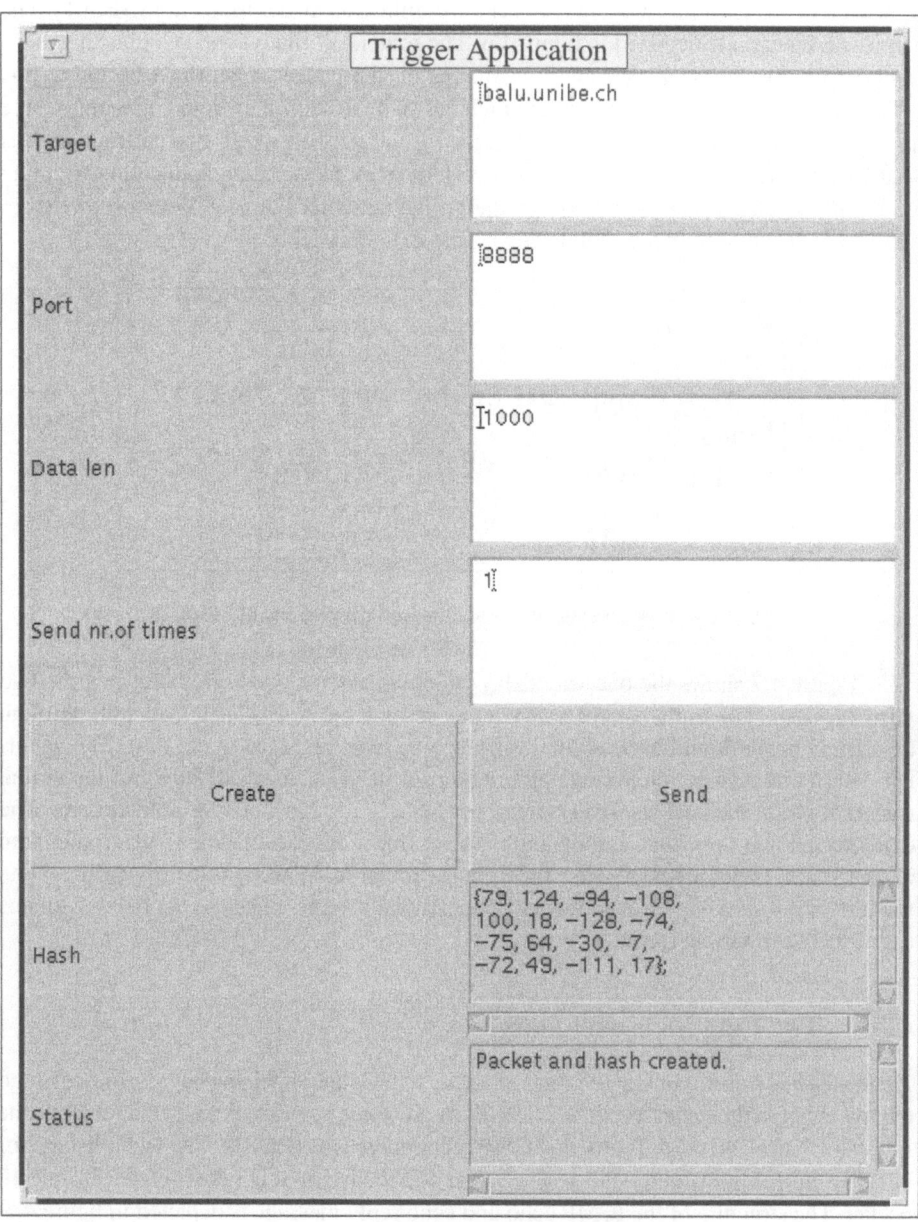

Figure 4.5: The trigger application.

a precise clock synchronization service was beyond the scope of this work, we used virtual routers [BB00] to emulate a network. Note that another possibility would have been to use clock synchronization and clock skew elimination as described in [SBBS01]. The deployed scenario is depicted in figure 4.6. The routers all run on one PC, thus they have access to the same clock. So, the time-stamps on the packets monitored by the agents all refer to a single clock. The scenario includes two virtual routers interconnecting three private networks. The PC is connected to the virtual networks with two softlink devices that have the same look & feel as real network devices. Networking applications running on the PC can send real traffic through the virtual network. For each virtual router there is a CSM node that provides monitoring access to CSM agents.

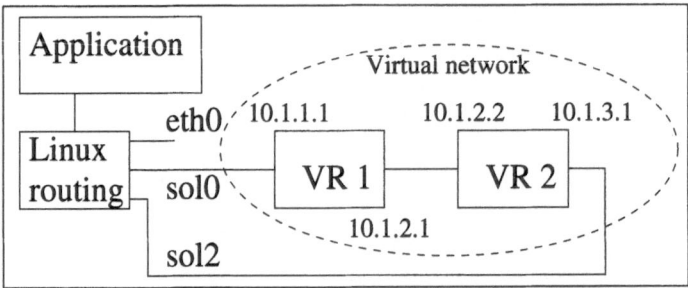

Figure 4.6: A measurement scenario with two virtual routers.

Figure 4.7 shows the one-way delay (in *micro*seconds) measured between the two virtual routers. The traffic source was a telnet session that was routed over sol0, through the virtual network and back to the host machine over sol2 (see figure 4.6). The agents use a hash that matches an average of 1 in 16 packets. It can measure how fast the virtual routers forward the packets. Every delay was clearly smaller than 0.6 milliseconds. The delay variation is nevertheless quite high. This is due to the fact that the virtual routers run in user space. Other processes may preempt the router and interrupt the forwarding. Note that the one-way delay measurements can easily be used to calculate the delay variance (jitter) between virtual routers.

4.3.4   The Ping Measurements

As mentioned before, the agents may possess knowledge of higher layer protocols and exploit this for their measurements. The *Ping Listener* agent uses knowledge about the Internet Control Message Protocol (ICMP) echo messages [Pos81]. The agent listens for ICMP echo (request) and echo replies. One ICMP message is encapsulated in one IP packet. The structure of the ICMP echo and echo reply message is depicted in figure 4.8. The ping listener agent records the arrival times of the requests and of the corresponding replies. The agent can perform a correct mapping by using the ICMP *identifier* field to distinguish between different sessions and the *sequence number* field to map a request to a reply. Note that the agent can be used passively. It will then provide results each time

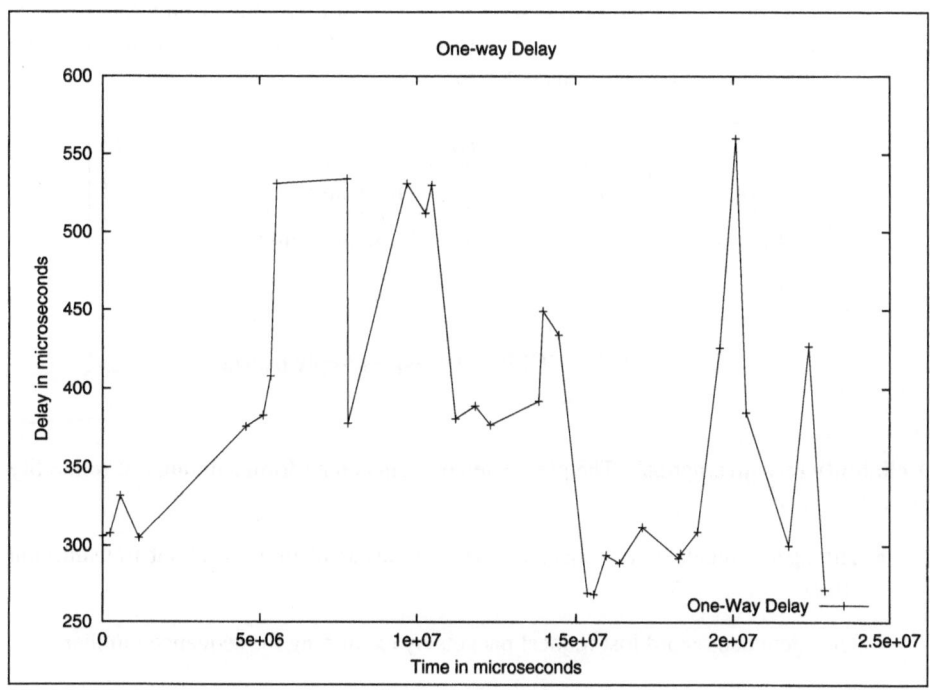

Figure 4.7: One-way delay between two virtual routers.

somebody starts an ICMP echo session, e.g. by running the ubiquitously used software tool Ping.

The ping listener agent groups the measured ICMP messages into series of configurable length (typically 10 requests and corresponding replies). For each series it reports a result statistics back to the home application. The agent can be configured to collect an arbitrary number of series. The following paragraphs outline how the agent collects the contents of these reports: reliability measurements, jitter, and delay information. Note that several ping listener agents can be located on a test path. Thus, more information is gained between a sender and a receiver compared to a classical active measurement. For example, if some agents see an echo message but the echo does not reach the sender, then the loss producing part of the path can be identified. In a traditional ping-based active measurement scenario (see section 6.2.3) we cannot distinguish between such an echo loss on the path and the failure of the receiving host.

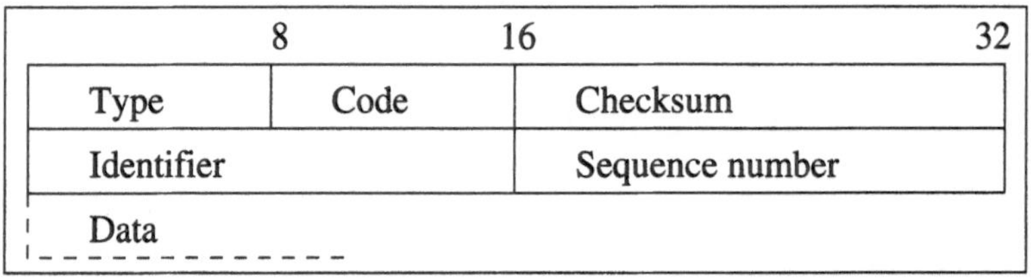

8	16	32
Type	Code	Checksum
Identifier		Sequence number
Data		

Figure 4.8: The ICMP echo request/reply packet.

Reliability measurements.   The ping listener agent can perform a number of reliability measurements:

- The agent calculates the checksum (if it is used) to find out about transmission errors.

- The agent can record lost request packets by examining the sequence number.

- The agent can record how many replies were lost.

- The agent detects packet duplications.

- The agent can record requests or replies that are sent in a wrong order (packet re-ordering in the network).

Jitter.   The ping listener agent is able to calculate network traffic delay jitter. It can, for example, compare the delays between a request and a corresponding reply and calculate the standard deviation. This jitter sums up the delay variation introduced by the downstream portion of the round-trip path plus the execution time of the ICMP stack. If we assume that the ICMP echo application sends the requests in regular intervals (e.g. ping can be told to do so), then the jitter introduced between sender and the measurement

point can be measured separately. For this purpose the agent compares the time between
the arrival of the consecutive packets and calculates the standard deviation to report it to
the home application (see section 3.6). Figure 4.9 shows the delay variations measured
by the ping listener agent. The agent resides on the virtual router V1 of figure 4.6. The
tests used the ping application to generate an endless sequence of ICMP echo requests
targeted at the virtual router V2. The application generates one request per second in regular intervals. The agent used a series length of 10 (10 consecutive messages were treated
as a group), thus per group there are 9 delays. Each delay is compared with the previous
in order to measure the jitter depicted in figure 4.9. In general the jitter was very low
(about 0.03 milliseconds). However, at some times there are large deviations (here about
4 milliseconds). This is the same phenomenon as already measured by the one-way delay
agent (see section 4.3.3) and is due to the fact that the virtual routers run in user space.

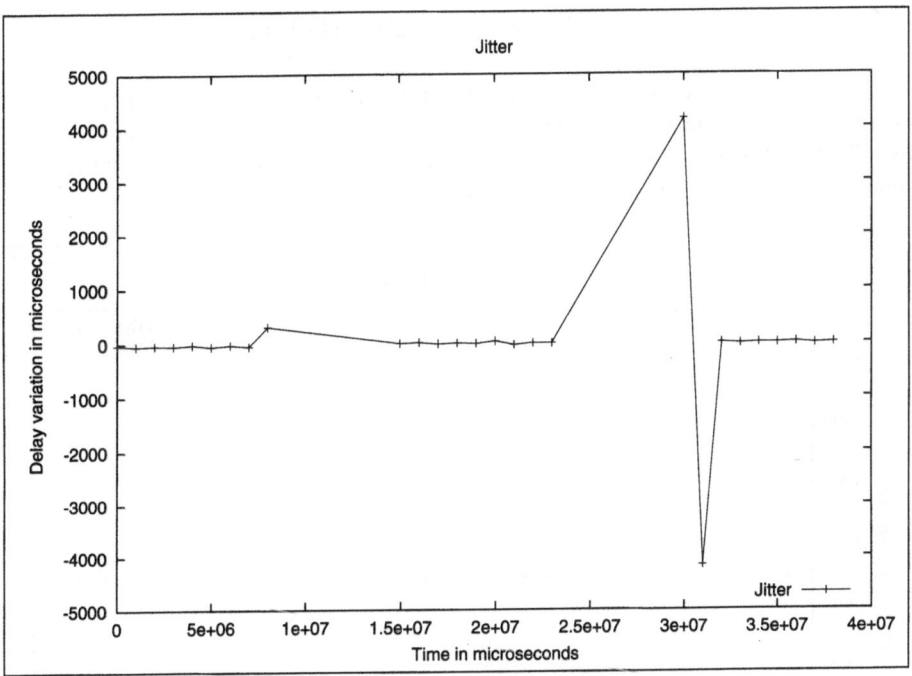

Figure 4.9: Jitter measurement in a virtual router.

Round-Trip Delay.   If there is no synchronized clock available, the ping listener agent
cannot measure how much delay a single packet has gained since the last measurement.
Still, the agents can provide a more fine-grained picture of where packets are delayed in
the network. The agents do not need a synchronized clock to compare the time between
a request and a reply. The agents on the path can thus measure *partial round-trip* times
(see also figure 4.10). The difference between the partial round-trip times measured at

two adjacent nodes is equal to the echo traveling time (of both the request and the reply message) in the intermediate network. While the agent cannot determine if it was the request or the reply packet that caused more delay, it can figure out which provider network causes the largest part of the round-trip delay.

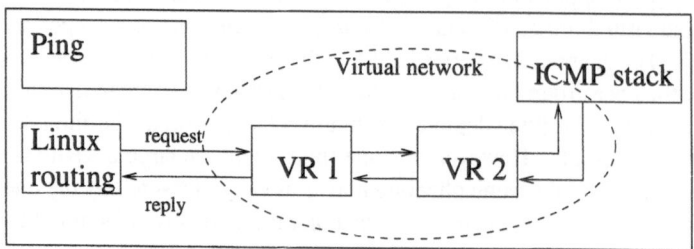

Figure 4.10: Measuring partial round-trip times.

Figure 4.11 shows the partial round-trip times measured in the setting depicted in figure 4.10. We see that the second router causes relatively little delay with little jitter. Its ICMP stack is obviously fast. The round-trip time measured by the second router is significantly larger and the traffic suffers from more delay jitter.

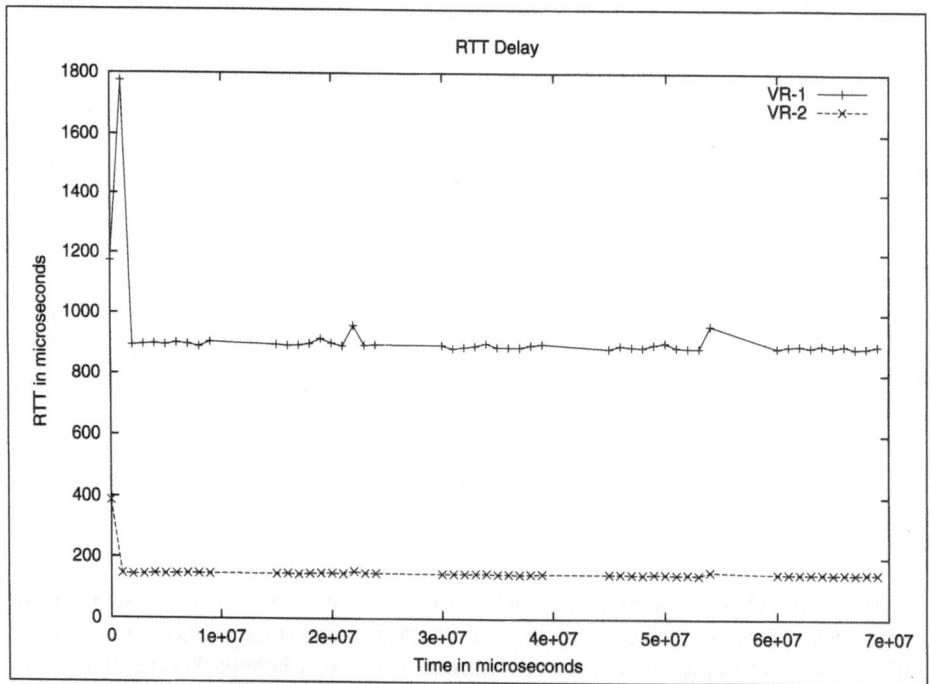

Figure 4.11: Partial round-trip times of two virtual routers.

Impact of cross traffic.   The tests described here use the same scenario (figure 4.10). The tests will prove the ability of the ping listener agent to detect the influence of cross traffic and congestion on the round-trip time and on traffic loss. This time the pings are directed to the outbound interface of V1. In order to produce congested links, we used the UDP sender application presented in [SBBS01]. The link capacity of the virtual network is shaped by a token bucket filter to conform to an average of 1 Mbit per second. Figure 4.12 shows 5 series of ten round-trip times for an uncongested network. Figure 4.13 represents the round-trip times when the virtual routers have to forward a background traffic of 1 Mbit per second. Still, there is no packet loss but the delays increase heavily. Figure 4.14 shows the delays with regard to background traffic of 3 Mbit per second. Some ICMP messages still get through but there is a heavy loss, too. Note that the loss is not explicitly depicted in the graphs but it can be seen as missing RTT bars. The heavily congested network in figure 4.14 shows only 29 out of 50 RTTs, so 21 ICMP messages were lost.

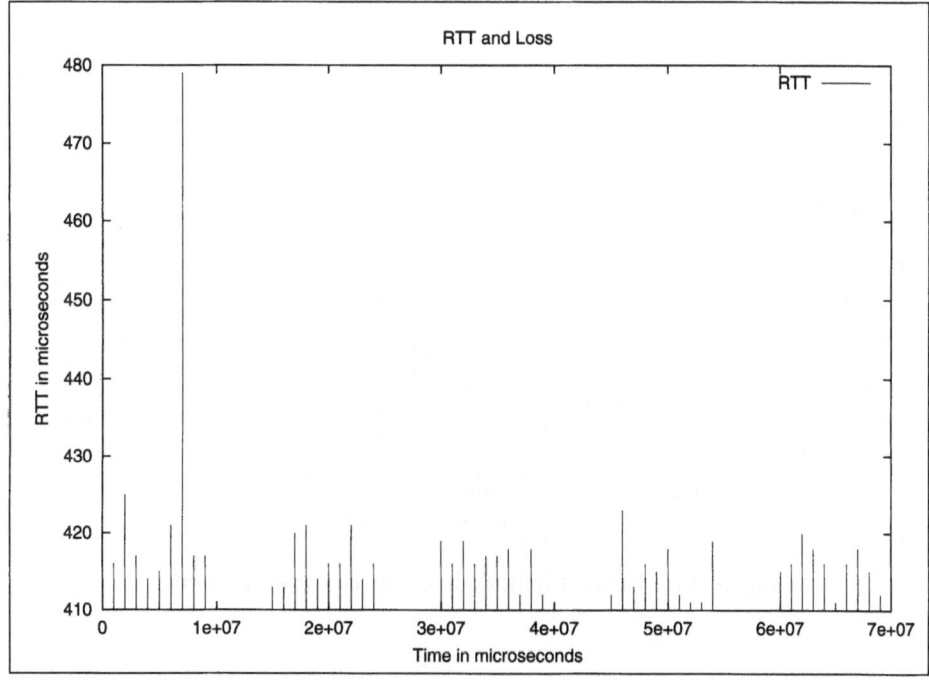

Figure 4.12: Round-trip times in uncongested network.

4.4   Agent Security

The CSM infrastructure protects the CSM node, the monitored device, and traffic from illegal access by the agent. In addition, agents are protected from each other. This sec-

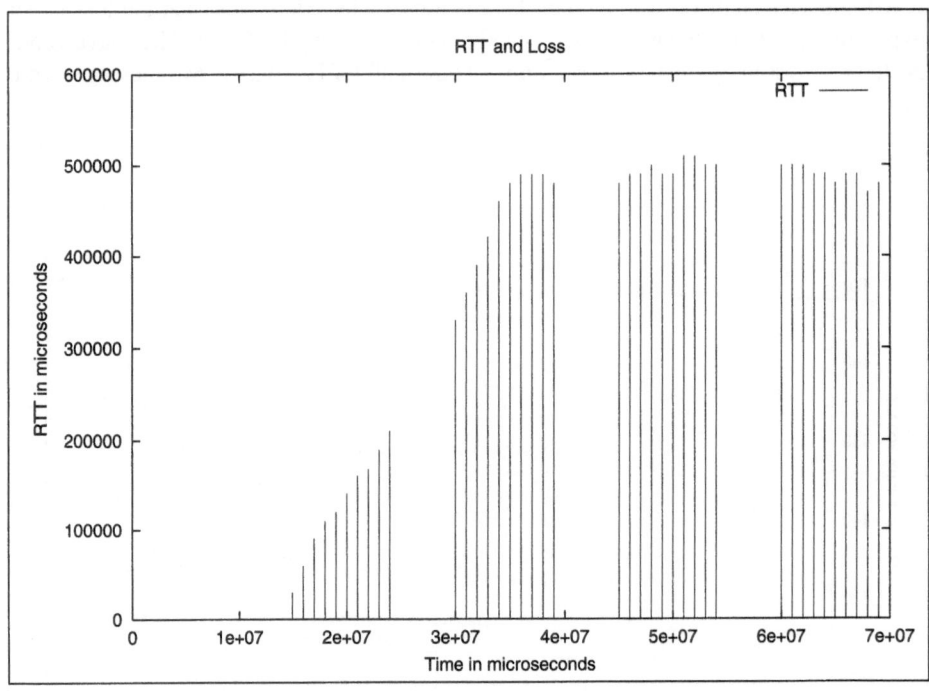

Figure 4.13: Round-trip times in mildly congested network.

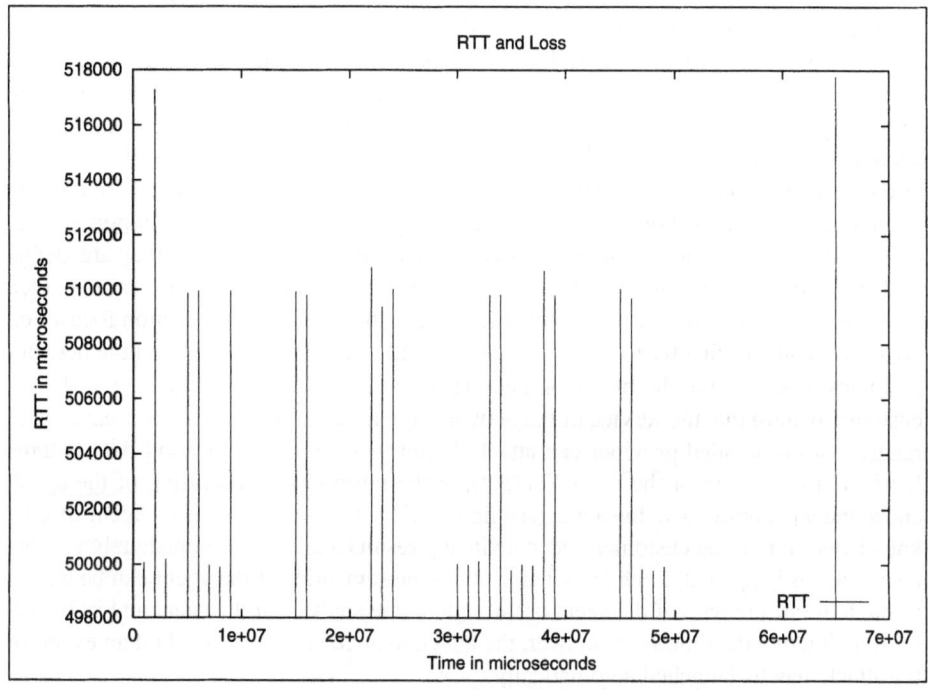

Figure 4.14: Round-trip times in heavily congested network.

tion discusses attacks that are launched by the provider against an agent in one of the provider's CSM nodes.

4.4.1   Classification of Attacks

The agent is protected against exterior attacks from foreign providers or customers. Yet, the agent fully depends on the benevolence of its execution environment. The usual approach to protect the agents from the execution environment is to let the agents run in a secured box of a trusted third party. This approach is not appropriate for CSM because the providers will probably not allow a third party to install a network measurement tool at the provider's premises without giving the provider full access. So, we have to live with the assumption that the provider has full access to the CSM node. This section is not going to discuss denial-of-service attacks launched by the execution environment. The node can, for example, refuse to deliver packets to the agent, refuse to execute the agent, kill the agent before its normal termination, and refuse to send results of the agent. It is the right of the execution environment to deny services. This is necessary, for instance, in order to enforce resource control or to provide better services for agents of more important customers. Denial-of-service 'attacks' do not deceive the customers, because they are visible to them. If the customer is not satisfied with the service that his/her agents receive, then the customer can reconsider the business relation to the provider. This section focuses on goal driven attacks that try to manipulate the monitoring results in order to hide network problems or worse, put the blame on peering network providers. Such attacks make the customer believe that the service or the network is in a state other than in accordance with reality. An ill-intended provider can attack the integrity of the monitoring data at three levels: at the sending of the result (output), at the information processing of the agent, and at the input delivery to the agent (see figure 4.15). The attack may need agent specific knowledge so that the customer gets convincing results and cannot immediately see that an attack has happened. Such knowledge about the semantics of the agent can be gained through offline analysis of the agent or through online analysis of the agent and its behavior (e.g. internal dataflows). Moreover, the attack may be launched by a human expert or the attack may be launched automatically.

Here are examples of these attack types:

- **Attacking the output of the agent.** The attacker may for example see that the agent sends status reports containing fields labeled with 'bytes per second' and change the value of this fields to his/her liking. In general, the attacker must know (1) what the agent measures and (2) how the results are formatted and (3) when they are due.

- **Attacking the agent processing.** The attacker may, for example, remove commands that trigger alarms which would inform the customer that his/her service is broken. The attacker may start a harmless version of the agent instead of the agent sent by the customer. For such an attack the attacker must have detailed knowledge about the semantics of the agent.

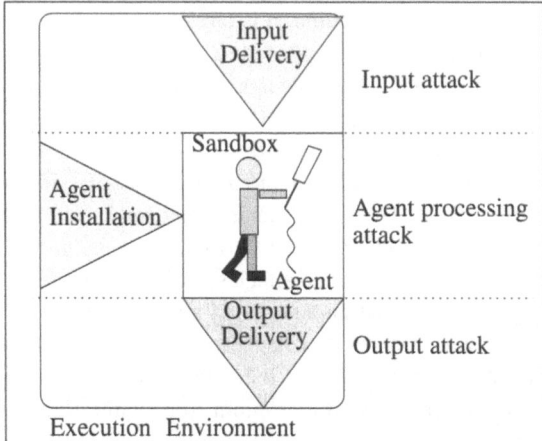

Figure 4.15: The three attacking targets.

- **Attacking the input of the agent.** The node may, for instance, simply not deliver those packet copies that reveal a problem. Another possibility is to manipulate the timestamp of the packet copies. The attacker may deliver packet copies that originate from other locations than the monitored network device. This attack may also work without knowledge of the agent semantics.

Unfortunately, manipulation of the agent or its result cannot be stopped. For security reasons, agents need to be under full control of the executing node. The node environment must be able to interpret the agent's bytecode so that the agent functionality is performed correctly. Note that some agent platforms rewrite the bytecode of every agent in order to enforce resource control [BHV01, VB99]. So it is always relatively easy for the node to manipulate the agents, but we will show that the ability to program agents in a general purpose programming language is a powerful tool in order to sooner or later detect unannounced tampering with the agent. Our goal is to prove that the customer can write agents which are so hard to manipulate that it is actually much easier and more cost effective for the provider to (re)engineer the network to accommodate the promised service than to try to cheat.

4.4.2 The Semantics of the Agent

If the attacker wants to fake a meaningful agent result, then the attacker must know the intention of the agent. For normal CSM agents this may work as follows: the attacker decompiles the agent and reverse engineers it. By analyzing the agent source code the attacker can deduce what the agent is supposed to measure. The attacker includes a cheat mode into the nodes that automatically performs a manipulation each time this agent is sent again. For example, the sending service may rewrite results or instead of the original agent a fake version is started. This is a human driven attack. Because humans are involved, the initial attack has to be offline. It is obvious that no human can reverse engineer any agent faster than the agent is supposed to start sending results (within seconds). On one hand it is hard to protect the agents against offline human driven attacks, but on the other hand it is not necessary to provide a bullet-proof protection against such an attack since the attack effort is too high. Note that the attack-taskforce of the ill-intended provider would have to be ready all the time to analyze and classify every agent that every customer, peer provider or third-party vendor may send. Yet, if the attack could be automated so that the agent is attacked on the fly, then an ill-intended provider may profit from the deployment of such an automated attack system. Nevertheless, computing theory gives us a convincing argument that an automated attack working for all kind of agents is not feasible. As mentioned before, the attacker must know about the semantics of the agent. Yet, the agent is a complete program. It can be proven that there exists no program that is able to determine in finite time if a program stops within finite time (the infamous halting-problem [Tur36]). So from that we can extrapolate that there is no program that can extract the semantics of all other programs.

Of course, in practice things look different because the attack program does not have to work for all agents. It is enough if it works for most agents. Yet, reverse engineering is a hard problem and current tools struggle to analyze the structure of a program and do not even try to extract semantics. Thus, automatic (online) attacks on the CSM agents are not feasible given the state-of-the-art of artificial intelligence.

CSM agent programmers can also make the offline analysis by humans hard. Here are some measures that can be taken that discourage the reverse engineering:

- **Obfuscated code.** Obfuscated agents include unnecessary entities in their byte-code such as additional variables, calculations, branches, functions, and classes. The agent developers should make sure that all of them are used in some cases and influence (unnecessary) parts of the result so that smart compilers cannot remove the obscure parts. The format of the result should also be obscure. For example, the result may be split in parts. Numbers may be transformed with bijective functions, like in the case of floating point results where the multiplicative inverse may be sent. The designer of obfuscated agents can exploit the expressive power of a full-fledged programming language to create endless variations of an agent.

- **Non-trivial filters.** Obfuscated agents should use filters that match more packets than actually needed and re-filter the packets internally. Otherwise, the attacker may guess the intent of the agent based on the requested monitoring traffic.

- **Obfuscated boolean expressions.** Internal filters can be protected, too, by using obfuscated boolean expressions. Here is a generic way to do so: (1) Use a tautology generator to create an arbitrary number of tautologies T_i out of many variables of the agent. A tautology T is a boolean expression that always evaluates to true no matter what the values of the involved attributes are. Tautologies can be created in linear time. (2) Use a generator that analogously creates boolean expressions that are always false F_i. (3) Obfuscate the filter expression B by generating an equivalent expression through random iterations of the following rules: replace B

with $T_i \wedge B$ or $B \wedge T_i$ or $F_i \vee B$ or $B \vee F_i$. The resulting expression is equivalent and much more complex than the starting expression.

- **Send meaningless agents.** Instead of including meaningless functionality the customer can sent entire agents that do not calculate anything useful. If such an agent starts sending useful results, then this is a good sign that some tampering has taken place.

- **Using the input.** The agents may use the packet copies to dynamically change their behavior. A simple instance of this approach is the trigger agent (see section 4.3.2). The agent may apply an arbitrary (possibly secure) hash function to each packet and treat only those packets that match a certain hash value. The customer may extrapolate the service state from the state of that particular subset of the traffic. The trigger agents themselves are relatively easy to reverse engineer. Yet, the hash mechanism may be used to construct a meaner obfuscated agent: Such agents *interpret* the payload of packets that match the hash functions. The data in these packets may describe a permutation of input variables. Before the permutation is known, the attacker cannot analyze the calculations that base on these input variables. Moreover, the agents can interpret parts of the payload of these packets as commands. Imagine an agent that implements a stack machine. It places its input variables on a stack according to an order described in a matching packet's payload. It interprets further parts of the payload as operations such as addition, multiplication, division, etc. The attacker would need to break the hash function in order to see what kind of packets match and thus trigger the calculation. Instead of a stack machine, the agent may itself be a virtual machine. This idea is used in [Tsc99] to securely end distributed services in an active network. The agent validates the packet with the secure hash function. It then executes the contents of the packet as commands.

- **Mobile Cryptography.** Mobile cryptography is defined as the study of mathematical techniques related to aspects of information security of mobile executable code in a network [ST98]. The basic idea is to encrypt executable code in a way that the code can still be executed. More specifically, the agents use *encrypted functions*. Be f a function with $f(x) = y$ then we denote $E_f(x)$ as the encrypted function of f. E_f will have the following properties: (1) it is computationally hard to find the function f given E_f. (2) $E_f(x) = E(y)$ thus the encrypted function delivers the encrypted result of the function f. Say that the customer wants to execute the function $f(x)$ remotely and obtain the result y. The remote execution environment shall neither be able to understand the function f nor to see the result y. Given encrypted functions, the customer calculates E_f and generates an agent $A(E_f)$ that implements the encrypted function. The customer sends the agent which is then executed in the node. The node executes $A(E_f)(x)$ and delivers the result $E(y)$. The customer then decryptes $E(y)$ and thus gets the desired result y. The node only sees the encrypted function and the encrypted result. Therefore, mobile cryptography could completely conceal the semantics of the agent. Unfortunately, until today no algorithm to generate generic encrypted functions exists, and it is not proven that a secure algorithm exists at all. [ST98] proposes an encryption method E and an algorithm that can compute $E(x + y)$ from $E(x)$ and $E(y)$ without revealing x or y. Furthermore, they propose an algorithm to calculate $E(xy)$ from $E(x)$ and y without revealing x. The algorithm allows the agent designer to create encrypted functions for polynomial functions. Yet, the proposed encryption scheme E has been successfully attacked.

4.4.3   Attacks on the Input of the Agent

If the ill-intended provider knows about a network problem, then the provider may use attacks on the input of the agent to hide the problem. The 'nice' thing about this attack is that it does not necessarily require knowledge about the semantics of the agent.

In the situation depicted in figure 4.16 provider B has a provisioning problem and loses reserved traffic within B's network. The agent measurement results (the height of the bars show the throughput) clearly indicate the location of the problem. If B is ill-intended, aware of the problem, and has a clever intervention infrastructure on his/her CSM T-components, then B could launch the following attacks on the agent input: either it sends packet copies seen at B1 to B2 or it vice versa. The two variants and the subsequent measurements are depicted in figure 4.17. The black bars indicate the measurements based on the manipulated input. Variant 1 makes the customer believe that the traffic was lost on the link between A and B. Variant 2 makes the customer believe that the traffic was lost on the link between B and C.

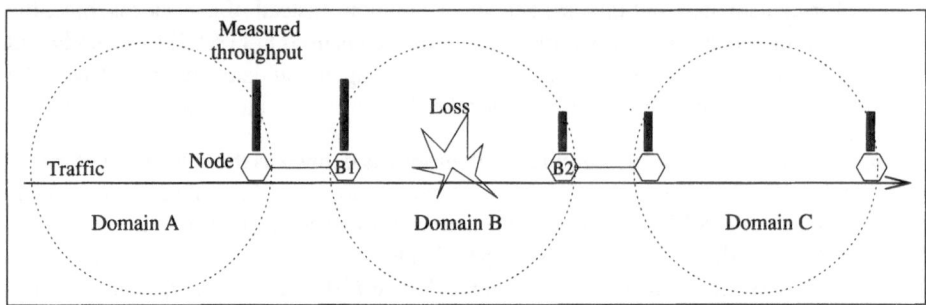

Figure 4.16: A loss situation measured at honest provider sites.

The mobility and the programmability of the CSM agents provide means to unveil the ill-intentioned scheme. The main problem for the provider is to keep the input to the agent consistent. The timestamps on the packet copy are already problematic. If the provider delivers the packets seen at B2 to B1, then the timestamp must be set back to an earlier time. But then, the agent may notice that it took the T-component much longer than usual to deliver the packets. The analogous problem may reveal the cheating when the provider delivers the packets from B1 to B2.

If the provider manages to calculate credible timestamps, then the customer has further means to unveil the cheating. Assume the cheating 1 variant of figure 4.17. For the

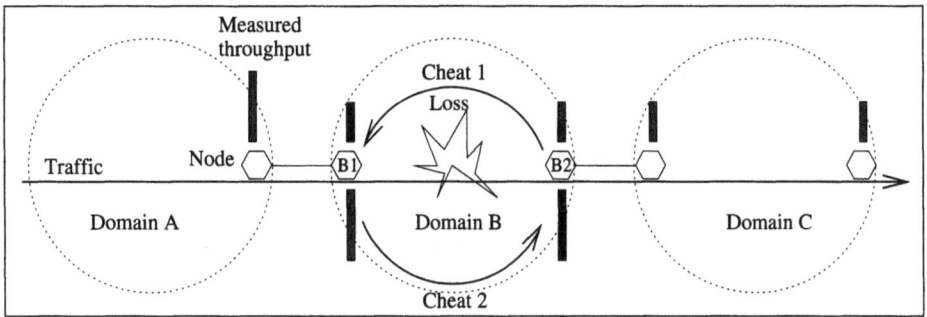

Figure 4.17: Two agent input attack variants performed by provider B.

customer it may be undecidable whether A has applied the cheating variant 2 or B has applied the cheating variant 1. The customer could then assign 'penalty points' to both providers. If later a similar situation occurs between provider B and C, then B would already have two penalty points which would indicate that B is probably cheating, and not A or C. The customer can also send further agents that surround the suspect providers. Measuring traffic delays and also delays within the CSM nodes (in similar ways as for the performance tests in chapter 5) generate further clues on who is cheating. Finally, the customer can perform active tests. The customer may, for example, generate and measure bidirectional traffic, or traffic from sources so that the traffic crosses only one of the cheating candidates. In case nearby CSM nodes provide a sending service without destination restriction, then the customer can send agents to exploit this service to test particular distrusted nodes.

4.4.4   Evaluation of the Threat Situation

¿From the discussion in this section it should be clear that today there is no bullet-proof solution that protects mobile agents from an ill-intentioned execution environment. However, it should also have become clear that the more effort the CSM agent developer puts into obfuscating their agents, the more resources the attacker needs to find out about the intent of the agent. Compared to stationary approaches, such as SNMP, this is a major improvement. There, the provider formats the results according to globally known semantics (MIBs). If the customer requests information from the provider (for example an SNMP get message), then it is immediately clear what the customer is looking for. Moreover, in static systems the customer can investigate the problem literally only from one side. With programmable and mobile agents ill-intended providers get involved in a 'race of arms' against the collective body of the customers. The ill-intended provider must always be aware of new agents that may reveal the cheating.

The following reasons underline the claim that in the long term no provider will profit from attacks against CSM agents:

- The agent developers can make it arbitrarily hard for the attacker to reveal the intent of the agent.

- The provider must allocate considerable resources and manpower for attacks against agents. The provider will profit more if this manpower is invested in the service provisioning.

- The more differently agents perform tests, the more difficult it becomes to manipulate these agents without running into consistency problems.

- The attacker must possess accurate knowledge about the state of the provider network in order to hide problems.

- An ill-intended provider is outnumbered by the customers. The provider faces the collective creativity of the customers, of peering providers, and of third party agent developers.

- There is always a chance that cheating is revealed. If so, the provider will probably face the full range of retaliation. Because of the aforementioned difficulties of launching an attack it is then obvious that the provider did it with ill-minded intent and cannot simply blame it on errors.

4.5   Extended Application Scenarios

The CSM infrastructure provides a generic interface for service monitoring. The metrics used by the agent depend on the service, on the customers' interests, and on the service level agreement between customer and provider. This section presents some more ideas for useful CSM agents and new node services that enable the agents to examine the new IP services more thoroughly.

4.5.1   Further Applications Independent of New Node Services

Customizable event notifications.   One important aspect of network monitoring is the notification of an authority (e.g. the system administrator) when exceptional networking conditions are measured. Today, event notification is often done manually (sometimes also referred to as trouble-ticketing). There, a formal way exists for the network users to report observed network problems. Automatic systems often use a threshold mechanism (e.g. SNMP traps) for event notification. If a network parameter is above or below a threshold, then a notification is sent. This model is useful but simplistic. If, for example, the network parameter stays very close to the threshold for a longer time or if it rapidly approaches the threshold, then issuing a notification or a warning may also make sense.

However, traditional stationary network monitoring infrastructures use a hard-coded notification mechanism (typically threshold-based). The CSM agents can decide for themselves when to notify and to whom to report. The agents can, for example, implement a heuristic model that notifies with a probability proportional to the proximity of the value to a threshold. They may thus implement a 'random-early notification' scheme. The agents can also use estimation functions that try to estimate the future (expected) measurement value based on the extrapolation of actual measurements [GB01]. Such a function may allow the agent to warn the customer early about problems that are brewing. CSM enables the customers to use the estimation function they think will serve their purpose best.

Trace-back of denial-of-service attacks. Distributed Denial-of-Service (DoS) attacks [CER99, Fer00] are able to knock out the network connectivity of even large e-commerce corporations. For launching a distributed service attack the hackers infiltrate a large number of systems that are weakly protected (e.g. because they belong to an open academic environment or because there is nothing interesting to be found on them). The hackers install software that allows them to direct traffic at the victim host. Because of the large number of traffic sources, the host under attack will be cut off from the regular traffic and may even crash. If the host provides critical network services such as domain-name lookup or proxy services, then an entire customer premises network may be affected by the attack. The DoS software sends IP packets with a forged IP source addresses. The victim is thus not able to trace the source of the attack and the hacker can use the installed DoS software as often as desired. A measure to prevent these kinds of attacks is described in [FS00]. At the network ingress points all traffic should be filtered. By consulting the routing tables the devices are able to detect packets with spoofed IP source addresses that are about to enter the Internet. Unfortunately, the deployment of such filtering rules may take a long time and there will probably always be sites that do not follow the rules. CSM agents are not intrusive so they cannot prevent distributed DoS attacks. However, they may detect the sources of the attack. Identifying the sources is very important since then the DoS software can be removed from infected systems and there is a chance that the hackers who installed the software can be located. The customer runs DoS detection agents which are sparsely distributed in the Internet. The agent performs sample testing of traffic destined for the customer network. If the agent has access to the node's routing (a node service), then it can detect spoofed IP addresses. If not, it can keep logs. Since not all DoS traffic is routed the same way, the agent is not affected by an attack. It can keep a log of unusually high incoming traffic. After an attack, the logs can be used to identify the path of the attack. The agent can also check back with the home application if there really is an ongoing attack. If so, the agent migrates to the next hop node over the interface from where the DoS traffic is coming. It then starts monitoring there, looking for traffic directed at the attacked host. Eventually the agent will migrate to the node nearest to the DoS attack source. Thus, even when the IP source address in the DoS traffic is spoofed, the agents can track down the source of the attack.

4.5.2   Future CSM Extensions

The expressive power of the proposed CSM architecture combined with the implemented node services is sufficient to perform the service monitoring tasks which are necessary for the proof of concept. This section presents some extensions that open even more possibilities.

Extended Node Services

Communication services.   The communication support available for a running agent is relatively restricted. Here are some additional communication services that the node may provide:

- **Injection of test traffic.** The agent may want to generate test traffic for active measurements. Some of the presented tests used specialized applications on the customer's premises, e.g. to generate traffic. If the agents can play this role, then the measurements are not restricted to end-to-end active measurements, thus they allow the customer to derive a more fine-grained picture of the service. In some situations it may even be useful that the agents insert traffic with spoofed IP addresses that appear to be coming from the customer's network so that downstream providers cannot distinguish between active measurements and 'productive' network traffic.

- **Reception of control traffic.** The control of agents may be simplified if they can use a node service to wait for commands from the home application. We can substitute this service by other techniques like the ones described in section 4.3.2.

- **Agent-to-agent communication.** For the presented CSM applications there is no necessity that the agents can communicate with each other. However, when agents are deployed in large scales, then an agent hierarchy may become necessary. With agent-to-agent communication manager agents have a way to control their subordinate agents (see also chapter 6.4).

When these communication services are implemented as node services, then the node should apply security measures. The traffic can, for example, be filtered in similar ways as the monitored traffic. The node can also enforce the traffic rates, e.g. by applying a token bucket filter.

Log file access.   Most providers keep log files about events that are relevant to the services provided. These log files represent aggregated information about the state of the service. For example, a VPN tunnel endpoint host may log the failed authentications or replay attacks. Introspection into these log files may save the customer a lot of monitoring work. The precondition is that the customer trusts these logs. The CSM agent infrastructure may be used to perform sample tests to verify the log files. If the CSM nodes provide a log files access service, then the agents can do this locally. Here is an example: the VPN implementation of Windows 2000 did under certain circumstances use the relatively weak

DES encryption even though it was configured to solely use the stronger Triple-DES encryption. This flawed behavior was visible in the log files [Vaa00, W2K00]. However, securing the log-file access may be more difficult than securing the traffic monitoring. The node needs policies that include knowledge about the semantics of the log files in order to decide whether an agent is allowed to browse through certain log entries.

A session key service. Section 4.1.2 showed that the quality of the provider's cryptographic algorithm may be examined by the VPN agents, but that there are limitations. By only examining encrypted traffic the agents cannot deduce which algorithm was used and with what key length unless it launches a brute-force attack. The nodes of VPN providers may thus offer a session key service. Only CSM agents that have proven through strong authentication that they were sent by a VPN customer may request the service. The node then delivers the currently used session key along with information about the applied encryption algorithm. The agent can now decrypt samples of the VPN traffic to check whether the decryption delivers a plausible result. For that purpose the agent may use knowledge about the sent plain text or it may, for example, recalculate checksums of higher layer protocols that were encapsulated. With such a session key service, the agent can therefore prove that the cryptographic algorithm in use is indeed the one specified and which key length was used. Note, however, that the node must be able to extract the session key from the current IPSec security association. This may introduce a security hole into the IPSec implementation.

Management information base access. Many network devices support simple network management information bases. Similar to the log file access the Simple Network Management Protocol (SNMP) allows the agent to collect information that is already condensed and thus more compact. For example, for measuring the network load the agent does not have to request copies of all packets. It might simply request the appropriate SNMP variable from time to time. Thus, it may be useful to introduce an SNMP management information base access service that offers support for (restricted) SNMP access to the monitored router. Handling (repetitive) monitoring tasks with local SNMP requests saves bandwidth and reduces latency. This has also been recognized by the IETF, therefore they developed an experimental standard for local management scripts [SQ99].

Model Extension

The customer-based service monitoring model described in chapter 2 is non-intrusive. In order to widen the application area, it can be useful to invalidate this property. Instead of requesting packet *copies* from the node, the agent may order the packet *originals*. The agent could then play a role in the forwarding process. The node would also offer a forwarding service and access to the routing table. Agents on such a node platform can obviously do more than just monitoring. They can shape traffic, implement a firewall mechanism and influence the route that packets take. They can also 'consume' certain packets, interpret the packet contents as commands, and possibly replace them with others. The CSM architecture would then become a full-fledged *active networking* platform (see section 2.2). The CSM protocol (see section 3.1) would then be the management plane of this active networking platform. This extension opens up new application areas that go beyond the customer-based service monitoring. However, the extended version of the CSM infrastructure is much harder to deploy because it is intrusive. This gives rise to new security problems and (probably even worse) it introduces performance problems. Note that the node environment cannot be physically separated from the router like proposed for CSM (see section 2.3.2). But even if the node environment is integrated in the routers, the Java agents are not able to perform forwarding at backbone link speeds.

Chapter 5

Performance Evaluation

This chapter provides an overview of the performance of the implemented customer-based service monitoring components. The focus is on the performance of the node environment but also the performance of relevant agents, the end-to-end performance as well as the T-component are discussed.

Methodology. The node environment runs (if not mentioned otherwise) on a Sparc UL-TRA 5 with a 269 MHz CPU connected to a 100 Mbit Fast Ethernet. If the T-component is the subject of the test, then it runs on an IBM Thinkpad 380 ED with a Pentium(r) processor and performs live packet capturing. The Thinkpad is connected to a 10 Mbit Ethernet. If the T-component performance is not the subject of the test, the author used a T-component dummy that artificially generates monitored traffic and sends it to the node. Time is measured using Java's System.currentTimeMillis() system calls at appropriate locations in the code. If not mentioned otherwise, the time is taken on a single machine. Therefore, no clock synchronization is necessary. The time is represented in milliseconds. Bandwidth consumption and throughput is usually represented in bytes, kilo-bytes (KB), and mega-bytes (MB) per second. Note that we interpret kilo as 1000 and mega as a million (not 2^{10} and 2^{20}). In order to have a benchmark time, the author implemented the *FastestAgent* which is an agent with empty method bodies. Thus, the agent does not perform any work. It is therefore the fastest possible agent.

5.1 Performance of the Node Environment

Each agent is isolated in a separate execution environment which 'feeds' the agent with monitored packets (see section 3.3.3, especially figure 3.6). A receiver puts the packets coming from the T-component into a queue. The agent wrapper takes the packet out of the queue and hands it over to the agent. The wrapper runs in a special execution thread. This separation brings about security but it may also impose performance penalties because of the context switch between threads. Therefore, we wanted to measure the speed of the packet hand-over. We replaced the receiver with a packet generator with parameterizable speed. The generator runs in its own thread and fills the queue with packets. After a fixed number of packets n, the thread yields its execution so that the agent can process the packets. In the following results this is referred to as the number of consumers to producers $(1/n)$. The test agents include the aforementioned FastestAgent and a throughput measuring agent. The latter uses the IP packet length field to measure the throughput over one-second intervals. For each interval the agent sends a result message back to the home application. Here are the results of some relevant test runs.

5.1.1   Throughput of the Execution Environment

The packet generator produces packets of selectable size at a selectable speed. The throughput of the execution environment is measured in bytes per time unit and in packets per time unit.

The throughput measurements are influenced by the rate at which the receiver generates packets. In this setting the packets are produced as fast as possible. Yet, always after a certain number of packets the generator yields the CPU (`Thread.yield()`). In order to determine the weight of this influence, we conducted the following measurements: we varied the aforementioned rate at which the agent (FastestAgent) is given the CPU to process the packets from 1 (once for each generated packet) to 1/40 (once for forty generated packets). Note that a smaller rate than this does not make sense, because the queue can only hold 40 packets. Thus, after the receiver has generated 40 packets, it will block anyway. The packet size here is 1500 bytes. The test result is shown in the graph of figure 5.1. Rate 1 is not optimal. The high number of context switches between the threads slows down the execution environment. The rest of the rates (between 0.5 and 0.025) do not cause significantly different performances. In the tests of the rest of this section the rate is set to 0.1 where not mentioned otherwise.

The speed of packet processing of the execution environment is also influenced by the packet size. Figure 5.2 shows the throughput in packets per milliseconds (for both agents presented) in relation to the packet size. The upper performance limit is 13 packets per millisecond (for 40 byte packets). The aforementioned throughput measuring agent (an agent performing real work) comes close to 12 packets per millisecond. Naturally, the packet throughput decreases for bigger packets. For maximum size packets (65535 bytes - not depicted in the graph) the maximum throughput is 2.55 packets per milliseconds.

Figure 5.3 visualizes the same measurement data, but now we compare how many bytes per second are delivered. ¿From this point of view, the execution environment performs better for large packets. For the maximum size packets the throughput reaches more than 167 MB per second. For small packets (40 bytes) the throughput measured is 516 KB per second. Note that these numbers represent absolute upper limits.

Influence of the resource control.   During their execution all agents are subject to resource usage control (see section 3.5.3). Once a second a resource controller checks the CPU and memory usage of the agents. This work may slow down the node. By comparing

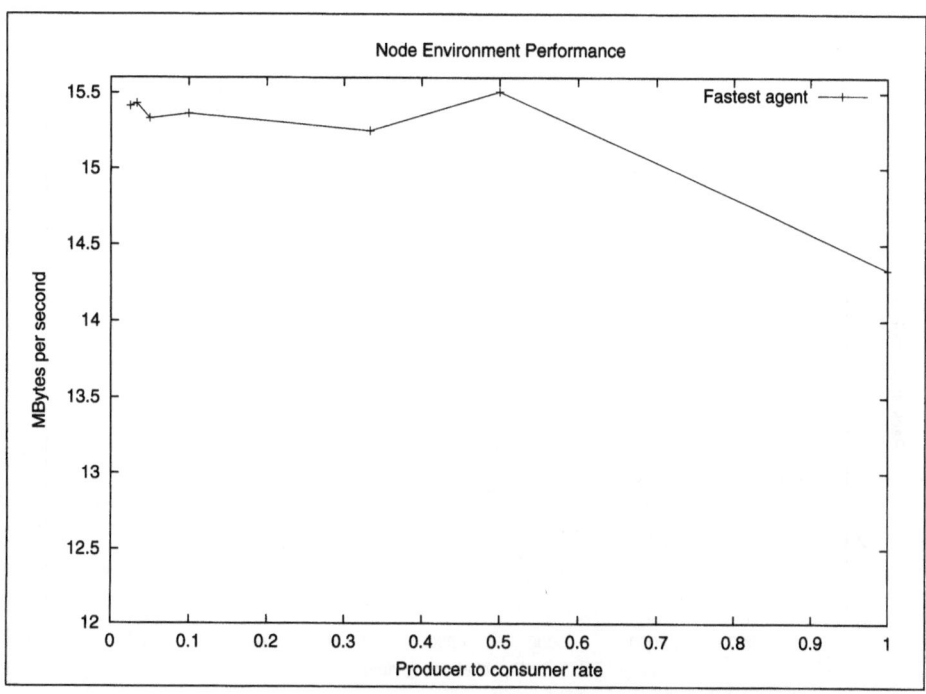

Figure 5.1: Influence of the packet generation rate.

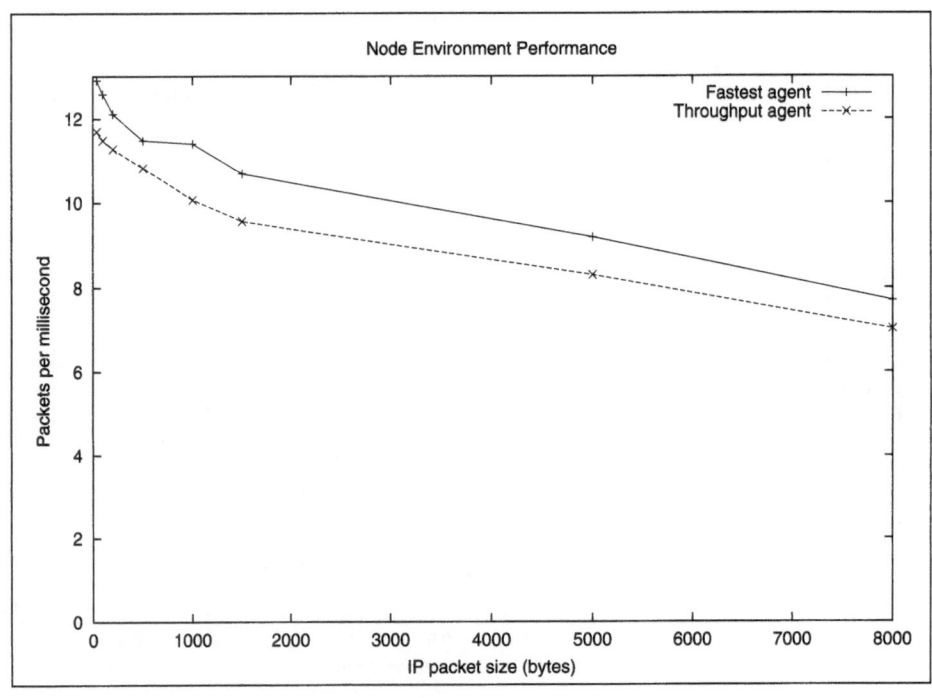

Figure 5.2: Packet throughput of the execution environment.

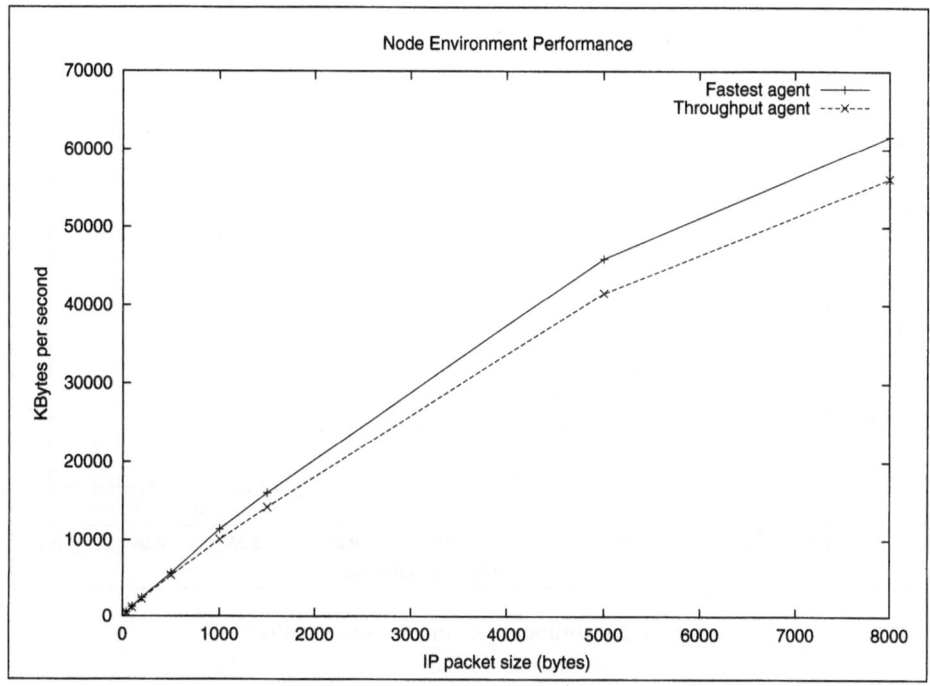

Figure 5.3: Packet throughput of the execution environment.

the performance of the FastestAgent with and without resource control, the impact of the resource control can be measured. The test run measured the time the execution environment needed to treat 100'000 packets with a size of 1500 bytes. The result is depicted in the graph of figure 5.4. Since the benchmark agent does not add overhead for agent specific computing, the impact of the resource control must stand out in this setting. Yet, as the figure suggests, the impact of the resource control is only minor (about 5%).

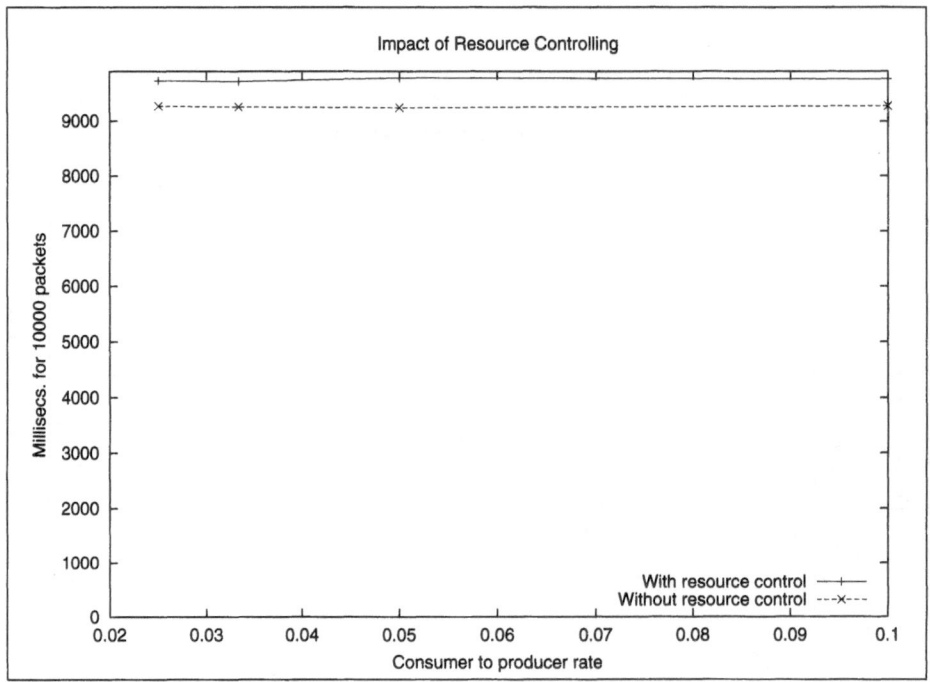

Figure 5.4: Influence of the resource control.

For regular agents that perform some work the relative impact is even much smaller. One exception is the memory usage control. The used mechanism (object serialization - see section 3.5.3) is relatively slow. Its effort grows with the size of the agent to be tested. We implemented a test agent that slowly grows in size. The CPU time used to determine its size during a resource check is shown in figure 5.5. The memory check duration is more or less linear to the size of the agent. Check times of larger agents tend to fluctuate more. Note that the graph ends at agent sizes of 40 KB because the node policy declares this to be the maximum tolerable size. The 300 milliseconds checktime for agents of about 40 KB size is large (about 30 percent of the interval time). Therefore, memory checks are not carried out at every check interval but only after a random number of intervals (again see section 3.5.3). This is justifiable because experiments showed that rapidly growing agents are usually eliminated by the CPU control mechanism.

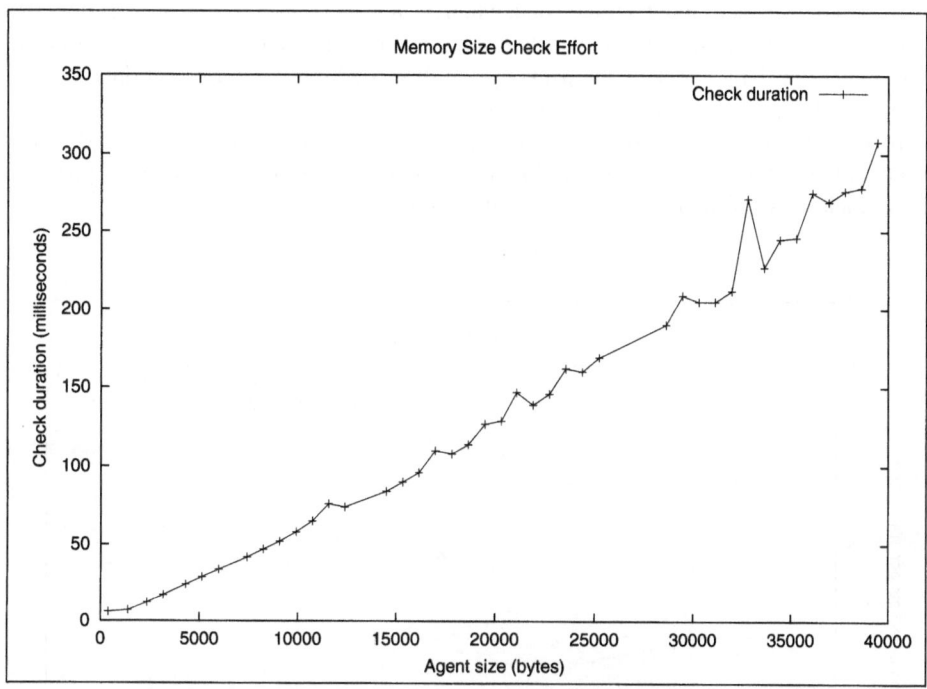

Figure 5.5: Size dependency of the memory control duration.

5.1.2   Node Throughput Including the TCP Receiver

In the previous experiments the receiver component of the execution environment generated artificial packets and injected them directly into the execution environment's in-queue. Here, a separate thread is used to emulate an external T-component. Thus, the monitored IP packets are still artificial, but they enter the receiver through a TCP connection. Again, the FastestAgent is a benchmark. In this measurement we vary the packet size to measure the impact on the packet throughput. Figure 5.6 shows the results. The throughput is again higher when the packets are bigger. The achieved throughput is now considerably smaller (about 5 times) than when the receiver generates the packets directly. This implies that the Java TCP/IP sockets are a potential bottleneck of the execution environment. For larger packets the packet per millisecond rate decreases yet only slowly. However, for packets smaller than 200 bytes there is an anomaly where small packets experience a smaller packet rate. This can have several reasons, for example, that the Java socket implementation for either sending or receiving is less effective for small packets. Nevertheless, we could not clearly locate the cause.

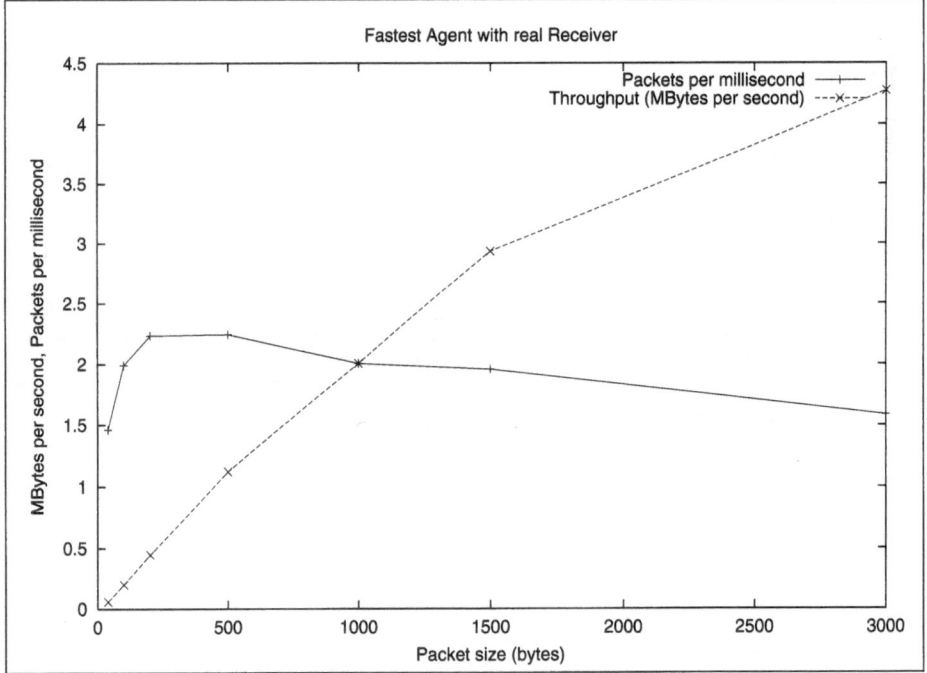

Figure 5.6: Throughput of the execution environment including the TCP receiver.

5.2 Agent Performance

The previous sections already presented the performance of the fastest agent possible and the performance of a throughput agent. The latter did perform close to the benchmark. It represents those agents that do only little work per monitored packet, such as agents for delay, jitter and loss measurements. This section discusses the performance of the VPN agent presented in section 4.1. The agent calculates statistics of the complete payload of the monitored packets. The VPN agent is therefore a performance 'heavyweight'. The VPN agent can perform two kinds of statistical tests: the byte-frequency test and the run-length test. The byte-frequency test involves more computation because it works on 256 value classes whereas the run-test only uses six classes (see section 4.1.2).

Each agent has an emergency method to treat packets if the in-queue is running full (see section 3.4). Usually, this method just discards the packet[1]. This is also the case for the VPN agent and thus such packets are referred to as 'lost' packets. The mechanism allows agents to treat packet bursts and continue their work even if the load of incoming packets is higher than the agents' packet handling capacity. This emergency mechanism is nevertheless limited. If the agent handles too many packets as emergency, then the node interprets this as a sign of a congestion and starts killing low priority agents (see section 3.5.3). Figure 5.7 shows the performance of the VPN agent. Here, the receiver acts as a packet generator with a varying rate (see section 5.1.1). A smaller rate means that more packets are produced before the agent is given a chance to consume them. The results show that the throughput stays relatively constant when less than 20 packets are produced before the agent gets a chance to consume them. After this stage the agent starts to drop packets. It can thus handle more packets and for this reason the throughput increases. The node limits the loss rate to 40 percent (0.4 in the graph). The VPN agent using the byte-frequency test is unable to support a consumer-producer rate of 0.025. Such a rate leads to a loss rate which is too high and owing to this the agent will be killed. The VPN agent using the run-test has a significantly higher throughput and can also support the generated traffic up to the maximum rate of 0.025. With a packet size of 1500 bytes, it can handle monitored traffic of up to 0.36 MByte (approximately 3 Mbit per second) without losing packets. This is also the maximum speed at which software devices can perform encryption. With a reasonable loss (less than 40 percent) the agent can support speeds of over 0.6 MBps (approximately 5 Mbit per second).

5.3 Communication Performance of the CSM System

¿From the perspective of the user the response time to an agent execution request is relevant. This is the time that elapses between the moment at which the user sends the agent and the moment when the user receives the acknowledgment that the agent is running. Note that the CSM protocol acknowledges the agent only after the execution environment is set up and the agent is started successfully. In the following test setting the CSM customer application runs on the same machine as the node environment. The requests

---

[1] The agent may also count these lost packets or perform a simplified test on them.

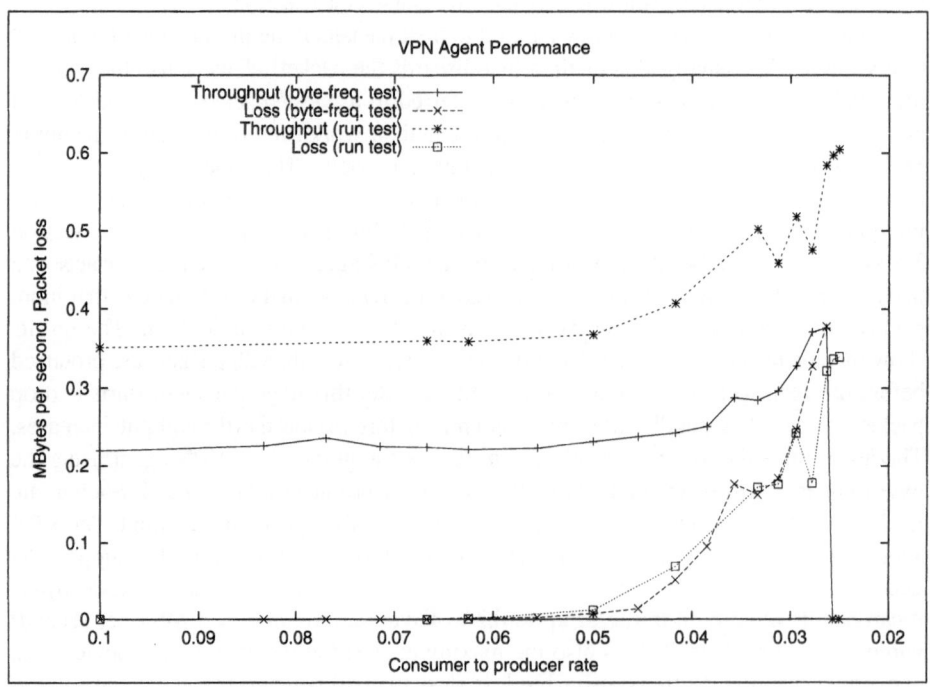

Figure 5.7: Performance of the VPN agent.

are sent through the local TCP/IP stack. The response time is influenced by a number of factors: the size of the agent, the encoding of the message, and the security overhead. We conducted a series of tests with ten samples each. The results for the benchmark agent (FastestAgent) are depicted in table 5.1. The first (minimal) option uses a receiver that generates packets and a node without resource control. The next option adds the resource control. The next series adds a real receiver with a TCP connection to a T-component dummy. This may impose some overhead because a server socket must be started for the communication with the T-component. The next step is to use PGP authentication for the CSM execution request messages. Finally, the response time for PGP authenticated and encrypted messages is measured.

Table 5.1: Response times of the FastestAgent

Option	Average (ms)	Standard deviation (ms)
Minimal	129.0	9.2
Plus resource control	126.2	7.8
Plus receiver	156.8	45.7
Plus authentication	1990.3	171.2
Plus encryption	3357.0	276.6

¿From table 5.2 we can see that the resource control does not have a negative impact on the response time. The start of a server socket for the T-component communication, however, has a small negative impact. Encryption and authentication add a large delay. Note that the node always answers in the same encoding as the request. So, not only the request is encrypted and decrypted (authenticated) but also the acknowledgment. Using the external PGP implementation has the advantage that the implementation is tested by many security experts and thus has become trustworthy and stable. Moreover, the computationally expensive cryptographic operations can be performed in native code instead of Java bytecode. Yet, as table 5.1 showed, the speed of the script-based PGP access (see section 3.5) is limited. Instead of a script-based approach, the Java Native Interface (JNI) can be used to access external PGP functionality [Jam01]. This improves the cryptographic performance. Nevertheless, the speed-up is not breathtaking. For small agents (1 KB) the speed-up factor is 1.71, for medium size agents it is 1.24 and for large agents (500 KB) there is no improvement.

The size of the agent has also an impact on the response time. The benchmark agent size is 692 bytes. The message of the execution request (which carries the agent and other information, e.g. the requested filter) amounts to 2154 bytes. The acknowledgment message size is 190 bytes. The VPN Agent execution request size is 29'238 Bytes. Table 5.2 shows the response time for a VPN agent execution request. The normal setting is with a real receiver and with resource control.

Table 5.2: Response times of the VPN agent

Option	Average (ms)	Standard deviation (ms)
Normal	179.9	64.5
Plus authentication	2864.8	267.7
Plus encryption	4505.4	193.4

Latency until the reception of the first result. The previously presented response times represent the time between the customer initiates the transmission of an agent and the time the acknowledgment of the agent execution returns (see also section 3.1.6). It is also interesting to observe how long it takes for an agent to send its first result. The sending of results is a node service, so it may be subject to additional latency (see section 3.3.4). To test this we implemented an agent that carries a payload of variable size. As soon as it starts executing, it sends this payload back to the home application. The agent performance can be compared with agents of other mobile agent platforms. We have chosen the NOMADS platform for comparison [SBB+00]. Table 5.3 demonstrates that the CSM platform outperforms NOMADS. This is mainly due to the fact that NOMADS uses a more fine-grained resource control mechanism and supports strong mobility. On the other hand NOMADS does not face the overhead of the T-component communication. Note that the execution platforms and the test layout were not exactly the same, so the results are only approximative. Yet, the tests showed that the performance of the CSM implementation does not significantly fall behind state-of-the art agent systems.

Table 5.3: Response times

Payload	NOMADS response (ms)	CSM response (ms)
0 KB	333.5	198.2
16 KB	337.4	273.4
64 KB	341.6	280.7

Latency within the CSM platform. The time between the generation of a packet at the T-component dummy and the notification of that packet at the home application is of interest because this is the minimum time that it takes an alarm to reach the customer. Figure 5.8 shows the latency measured. The scenario consists of one node which uses a dummy T-component that generates and sends artificial packets. The home application is running on the same machine. The time between the interception of the packet and the delivery of the packet to the agent is very short (usually smaller than 1 millisecond). The sending and reception of the CSM message (including object de-/serialization) takes about 55 milliseconds. This includes also the time that the agent's request to be sent waits in the service channel (see section 3.3.3).

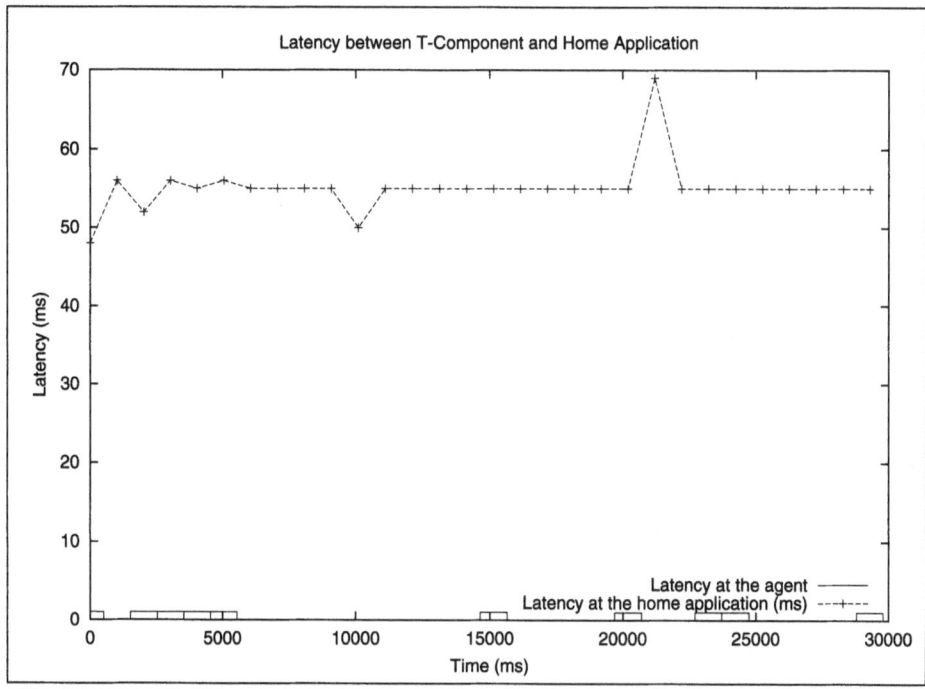

Figure 5.8: Latency between the generation of a packet, its delivery to the agent, and customer notification.

Forwarding Latency. The customer can request that the CSM agent be forwarded from one node to another (see section 2.4). For security reasons a node forwards only authenticated agents and only after the node could successfully start the agent. Therefore, the propagation of the agent will be relatively slow. A throughput measuring agent was used in the forwarding latency measurement setting. Figure 5.9 shows the test setting. There are four CSM nodes running in three machines on two different subnets. The CSM home application is also running on the machine named balu. The figure shows how the nodes are interconnected.

The first test run sent the agent to the node named IAM. The agent requested to be broadcast. Table 5.4 shows the resulting latency times. The numbers represent the time that has passed between the initial transmission of the initial until the call-back of the agent instance at that location. First the agent starts at the IAM node. After the execution this node sequentially forwards the agent to the RVS node, then to the CUI node and afterwards to the TIK node.

The second test sent the agent to the RVS node. The agent requested the node to broadcast it from there. The result is shown in table 5.5. Apparently, if a node has to

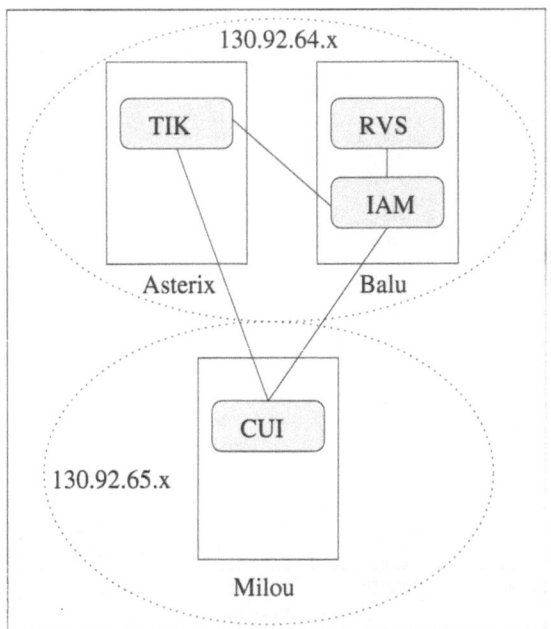

Figure 5.9: The forwarding latency test setting.

Table 5.4: Forwarding latency over IAM

Node	Latency (ms)
IAM	1520
RVS	2170
CUI	3827
TIK	5298

forward the agent to several neighbors, this slows down the forwarding. This is because the forwarding happens sequential. So, the node forwards the agent and waits for the acknowledgment before it forwards the agent to the next neighbor node. Furthermore, the node has to perform excessive cryptographic work when it has to authenticate the forwarding acknowledgments. An easy and effective optimization would be that the node forwards the agents in concurrent execution threads.

Table 5.5: Forwarding latency over RVS

Node	Latency (ms)
RVS	1515
IAM	2159
CUI	2778
TIK	4129

5.4 The T-Component

The previous performance measurements often used a T-component dummy to artificially create measured packets. This is to isolate the measured subjects (agents, the node, and the communication) from the influence of the T-component implementation. Now the focus is on the performance of the T-component that is capable of monitoring a real network device. The T-component implements the fast packet copy mechanism that delivers the input on which the CSM agents carry out their measurement. Thus, the T-component has to work at (a potentially very high) line speed. The task of the T-component is relatively simple. Therefore, the best solution would be to implement the T-component in hardware. Scripting was used to start the Tcpdump tool and a C++ program to send the output to the CSM node (see section 3.2). The T-component ran in a laptop with a 10 Mbit Ethernet interface. Using a laptop has the advantage that the network can easily be tapped at different locations but the disadvantage is that the laptop is relatively slow. The first version of the T-component was only able to forward traffic at a speed of about 0.75 Mbps. The main problems were that the C++ program parsed human readable Tcpdump output and that it sent the result in small chunks. The second version of the T-component uses the (undocumented) raw-format of Tcpdump and sends the copied packets in large chunks (ideally one packet per packet). In order to analyze the capacity of the new T-components, we used a UDP sender and receiver tool [SBBS01]. The receiver is located in the same machine as the T-component. The receiver measures how much traffic arrives at the laptop. The t-component copies the packets and sends them to the CSM node. The test scenario is shown in figure 5.10.

For the test packets of 1KB size were used. We compared the measurements of a throughput measuring agent with the results of the UDP receiver. Furthermore, we analyzed the CPU consumption of the T-component (the sender of the packet copies) and

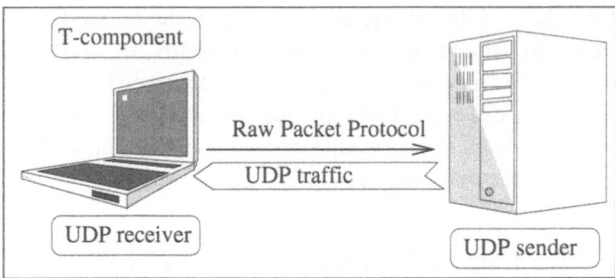

Figure 5.10: T-component performance test scenario.

of the underlying Tcpdump program. Table 5.6 summarizes the results. At speeds up to 4 Mbps the T-component did deliver all packets and the agent computed the correct throughput. Note that for 4 Mbps the CPU consumption of the T-component is already very high. At higher sending rates, Tcpdump consumes considerably more CPU time than before. The main problem is, however, the transmission of the T-component. The 10 Mbit Ethernet connection starts getting congested. The T-component sends back packet copies. It sends them wrapped in TCP packets which are wrapped in IP packets. So in theory the T-component more than doubles the traffic load on the Ethernet. As a consequence the TCP connection between the T-component and the CSM node (the raw packet protocol) suffers. The agent does not get all packets and measures a wrong throughput. Because the raw packet protocol backs-off the T-component blocks and yields the CPU, the T-component therefore uses less CPU in the congestion case. Tcpdump is able to cope with the traffic upcome, but it has to consume more CPU.

Table 5.6: T-component load

Sent	Received	Measured	T-component CPU	Tcpdump CPU
2 Mbps	1.95 Mbps	1.95 Mbps	<40%	< 5%
3 Mbps	2.92 Mbps	2.92 Mbps	<50%	< 6%
4 Mbps	3.85 Mbps	3.85 Mbps	<55%	< 20%
5 Mbps	4.70 Mbps	*3.20 Mbps*	<40%	< 25%
6 Mbps	5.60 Mbps	*2.00 Mbps*	<20%	< 30%

Nevertheless, the agent can request that the T-component only sends a part of the packet. When the agent requests only the first 40 bytes of each packet, then the T-component can support up to 6 Mbps without getting congested. For 7 Mbps the T-component is congested again. About 13 percent of the packets do not reach the agent. If packets are smaller than 1 KB, then the upper limit of supported traffic load is lower.

It is a UNIX pipe that delivers the dumped packets to the T-component. Thus, the packets travel a relatively long distance until they are finally delivered to the agent. Figure

5.11 shows this delivery time for the same scenario. The packet size is 1 KB and the T-component delivers a full packet copy. The UDP traffic load is 0.5 Mbps. The results indicate that there is a significant latency of about 300 milliseconds. Note that this latency does not influence the agents ability to measure correctly. The agent measures based on the timestamp provided by the T-component and not at the time when the agents first see the packet.

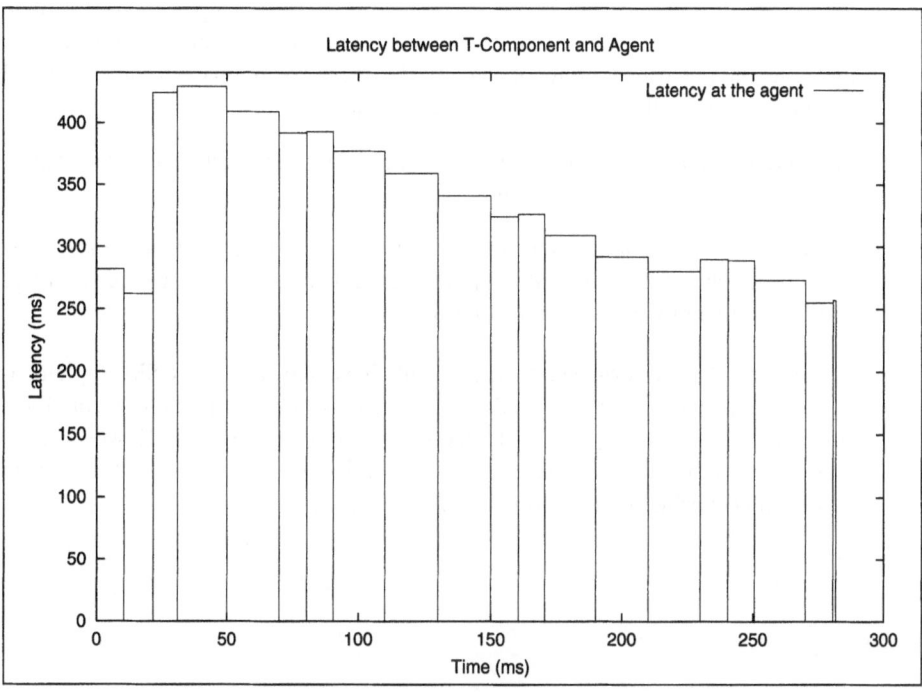

Figure 5.11: Latency of the Tcpdump-based T-component.

5.5 Discussion and Improvements

The purpose of the customer-based service monitoring architecture is to provide a facility for customers to measure the service level they obtain. All implemented components (node environment, agents, and T-component) support a data rate of at least 1.5 Mbps. Thus, the presented implementation can support customers with Frame Relay and T1 Internet connectivity. Yet, there are some shortcomings where the CSM implementation should be improved in order to accommodate higher speeds. Here is a summary of these shortcomings and suggestions for improvements.

- Instead of piping the Tcpdump output into another program the implementation of the T-components should directly access the packet capturing libraries. This will reduce the latency between the T-component and the agent. Backbone T-components should be implemented in hardware or at least directly in the monitored device to support higher network loads.

- The TCP/IP communication between the T-component and the node is a bottleneck. A UDP-based protocol with a checksum may be helpful.

- Small packets introduce significant overhead in both the T-component and the node environment. The problem occurs if the small packets are sent at a high rate. In that case, the raw packet protocol and also the agent execution environment should bundle several small packets into one packet/object.

- The cryptographic mechanisms are very time-consuming. Built-in cryptographic libraries may alleviate the problem.

- The object serialization mechanism is relatively slow. The byte stream it produces contains much redundancy. CSM applies the mechanism for the message protocol and for the memory consumption control.

Nevertheless, the performance measurements have shown that a CSM implementation is feasible in pure software together with off-the-shelf and portable technology. The implementation cannot support backbone speed service monitoring. However, even with security features included (authentication, encryption, resource control) the software implementation is capable of monitoring at WAN access speed.

Chapter 6

Comparison with Related Work

6.1 The Internet2 Initiative and the QBone

In 1996 several American universities started the Internet2 initiative [Rab98, Uni]. The Internet2 should recreate the partnership among academia, industry and government that fostered today's Internet in its infancy. The partnership aims at initiating the next evolutionary step of the Internet. Today, the Internet2 is a non-profit consortium, led by over 180 US universities and over 60 companies, developing and deploying advanced network applications and technology, thus accelerating the creation of tomorrow's Internet. The primary goals of Internet2 are to:

- Create a leading edge network capability for the American research community.

- Enable revolutionary Internet applications.

- Ensure the rapid transfer of new network services and applications to the broader Internet community.

The Internet2 is not a separate stand-alone network but it takes advantage of new high performance IP networks, such as the vBNS and Abilene. Abilene [ABI] is a US high-speed network spanning the USA with Sonet optical carriers OC-48 links (2404 Mbps). The Abilene is interconnected with CA*net 3 of Canarie [CAN], the Canadian counterpart of the Internet2, with the European research network TEN-155 [DAN] and other research networks around the globe. Abilene also peers with the very high performance backbone network service (vBNS) [vBN] of MCI. MCI runs the vBNS for the US National Science Foundation (NSF) until 2004.

The Internet2 members collaborate in working groups on advanced applications, middleware, advanced network infrastructure, and new networking capabilities. The last issue concerns the developing and testing of new IP network services and is therefore relevant to this book. In particular the QBone working group [Int99, THD+99] addresses

problems in connection with this book. QBone is an inter-domain testbed for differentiated services. QBone seeks to provide the Internet2 with end-to-end services in support
of emerging/advanced networked applications.

6.1.1   The QBone

Consistent with the Differentiated Services architecture, each network participating in the
QBone [Tei99] is considered a *DS domain* and the union of these networks - the QBone
itself - a *DS region*. QBone participants must cooperate to provide one or more inter-
domain services besides the default, traditional best effort IP service model. The first
such service to be implemented is a leased line like service called the QBone Premium
Service (QPS). Every QBone DS domain must support the Expedited Forwarding (EF)
Per-Hop Behavior (PHB) and configure its traffic classifiers and conditioners (meters,
markers, shapers, and droppers) to provide a QPS service to EF aggregates. Between
each QBone DS domain there are Service Level Specifications (SLS) that characterize
aggregate traffic profiles and per-hop behaviors to be applied to each aggregate. The SLS
is bilateral. Currently the QBone focuses on SLS for the QBone premium service and
refers to it as a globally well-known service. This simplifies the concatenation of bilateral
SLS into an inter-domain end-to-end service because the SLS can be designed so that
they 'fit' the QPS.

Today, the QBone consists of several DiffServ domains which collaborate to provide
end-to-end service guarantees. The QBone is thus a good example that illustrates the need
of a measurement and monitoring infrastructure for service management.

6.1.2   QBone Measurements

QBone participants must collect and disseminate a basic set of QoS measurements. Since
the QBone is a test environment it is important to posses complete measurement information in order to debug, audit and study QBone services. The QBone measurement
infrastructure is thus necessary to study and validate the operation of new DiffServ services and the application of these services. An important aspect of the measurements is
to verify that DiffServ traffic is indeed protected from other traffic according to the SLSs
in an end-to-end fashion.

The QBone participants must instrument each edge router of a QBone domain to
serve as a QBone measurement node (probe). Measurements are collected in three ways:
active, passive, and polling of static data.

- For active measurements the probe generates a small amount of test traffic and
  sends it to other nodes. Measured metrics are: one-way packet loss and delay variation. Also, complete trace routes are collected to test path stability.

- Passive measurements are used to derive the following metrics: traffic load in packets per second and bits per second.

- Polling of static data provides the following information which is used to interpret the other measurement data: link bandwidth, EF commitment (SLS), and EF reservation load.

All metrics should be measured for all existing behavior aggregates. The metrics must be applied simultaneously to the aggregates so that the results can be compared and correlated. This is important in the QBone context because one goal is to verify that the QPS traffic is successfully isolated from best-effort traffic. Therefore, a situation must be examined where the best-effort traffic suffers due to queuing-effects (e.g. loss or delay) but the QPS traffic is unaffected at the same time.

A large part of the QBone architecture describes the metrics and how the measurement data must be formated (e.g. in HTML) so that all QBone participants have access to a uniform database.

6.1.3 Comparison to our Approach

The QBone defines a uniform measurement interface to a uniform service. However, trust issues are not addressed at all. It is unrealistic that a commercial domain will make its complete measurement data available like QBone does. On the other hand, the advanced services will cost and thus the available measurements must somehow also become trustworthy. Furthermore, the QBone working group spent a lot of time and effort to specify the uniform measurement interface and measurement metrics. Still, they claim that new measurement metrics will be added as more experience is gained on this subject. Standardizing and deploying new metrics into all QBone measurement nodes is not a simple task. If the QBone deployed a customer-based service monitoring system as described in this book, then these problems could be solved more easily. A new measurement metric neither requires a standardization process of the working group nor a subsequent deployment of an updated QBone measurement node. The implementation and broadcast of a new measurement agent is all that would have to be done. In the initial QBone phases CSM measurement nodes could be open to anyone. Later, the security mechanisms of the CSM node (see section 3.5) can be used to restrict access to trusted parties. Finally, the mobile agent approach would help the domains to build trust into the remote measurements.

6.2 Network Measurements and Monitoring

In this section we focus on related work in the area of network measurements and network monitoring. In contrast to network monitoring there is also application monitoring. With this type of monitoring applications incorporate measurement code to monitor application specific behavior like hit counts of documents on a web server. Another example is the response time of a distributed system. The Application Response Management (ARM) API [ARM96] is an open standard for application monitoring. Yet, this section will focus on network management and on network related metrics because this is related more closely to customer-based service monitoring.

6.2.1   IP Measurement Methodology

Network measurement is by its nature a distributed task. Even the old but nevertheless useful `ping` tool needs a source and a destination (to reflect the ICMP message).

Here are distinctions of measurement approaches:

- **Active vs. passive measurements.** For active measurements additional traffic with known characteristics is injected into the network. Passive measurements work non-intrusively on the existing traffic.

- **End-to-end measurements vs. network element based measurements.** End-to-end measurements are carried out by the communication endpoints (sending and receiving hosts). Network element based measurements are also carried out within the network.

IP Performance Metrics

A network performance *metric* is a carefully specified quantity that is relevant to the performance and reliability of the network. The IP Performance Metrics (IPPM) Working Group has developed a set of standard metrics that can be applied to the quality, performance, and reliability of Internet services by networks operators, service providers, and other independent testing groups. [PAMM98] classifies metrics, specifies methodologies to collect statistics of the metrics and describes problems of measurement approaches (e.g. clock skew and unintentionally synchronized measurements). The performance metrics defined by this IPPM working group include: one-way packet loss across Internet paths (RFC 2680), one-way delay (RFC 2679), connectivity measures between two nodes (RFC 2678), and other second-order measures of packet loss and delay (RFC 2681).

Traffic Flow Measurement Architecture

The Real-time Traffic Flow Measurement (RTFM) Working Group has produced a measurement architecture to provide a well-defined method for gathering traffic flow information from networks and internetworks [BMR99]. This architecture can be applied to any protocol/application at any network layer. The proposed model is based on the concepts of *meters* and *traffic flow*. Meters observe packets as they pass by a measurement point on their way through the network and classify them into certain groups. For each such group a meter will accumulate certain attributes (such as the number of packets and bytes). These metered traffic groups may correspond to a user, a host system, a network, or a particular transport address (e.g. an IP port). Meters are placed at measurement points and selectively record network activity as directed by their configuration settings. Meters can also aggregate, transform and further process the recorded activity before the data is stored.

A traffic flow is a logical entity equivalent to a call or connection. A flow is a portion of traffic, delimited by a start and a stop time, which belongs to one of the metered traffic groups mentioned above. Attribute values (source/destination addresses, packet counts) associated with a flow are aggregate quantities reflecting events which take place between the start and the stop times. Flows are stored in the meter's flow table. Since there is no way for connectionless network protocols, such as IP, to tell whether a packet with a particular source/destination is part of a stream of packets or not, each packet is completely independent.

A traffic meter has a set of rules which specifies the flows of interest. Classifying packets into 'flows' provides a practical way to measure network traffic. Appendix C in [BMR99] offers a list of the flow attributes. Yet, there is no QoS related attribute specified.

Besides flows and meters, the traffic model measurement includes managers (to configure and control meters), meter readers (to transport recorded data from meter to analysis applications), and analysis applications (to process the data from meters readings so as to produce whatever reports are required). Since there has been considerable interest from users in allowing a meter to report on an increased number of flow-related measurements, the RTFM WG has produced a new document [HSBR99] specifying such measurements (the 'new' attributes). Some of the proposed extensions include QoS attributes, such as the DSCP to support DiffServ. Possible uses of the DSCP attribute include meters that aggregate flows applying the same code points, and that separate flows having the same endpoint addresses but using different code points. The new document also includes QoS parameters for Integrated Services based QoS support.

6.2.2   The Simple Network Management Architecture

To support and automate IP network management, the IETF standardized the Simple Network Management architecture (SNMP) [CFSD90, Sta99]. SNMP allows the monitoring of network elements and the pushing of configuration information into all kinds of IP-based networking devices. SNMP versions 1 to 3 exist. The older versions were mainly used for monitoring and less for configurations. The SNMP model provides an *SNMP manager* which is a management application that runs on a dedicated *management station* and is operated by the human network administrator. The manager communicates with *SNMP agents*. Each SNMP agent represents a local and permanent management process in a managed device. Thus, usually the network device implements the SNMP agent. The relevant device state is represented as SNMP objects (also referred to as variables). These objects are stored in a Management Information Base (MIB). MIBs have to be standardized in order to manage devices of different vendors. The language used to describe a MIB is called Structure of Management Information (SMI). It is a modified version of the Abstract Syntax Notation 1 (ASN.1) of the ISO OSI standard. The time between the specification of an MIB, its standardization, and finally the implementation of the MIB support in the devices is long (several years). MIB specifications for DiffServ and IPSec are underway. Yet, today only a (limited) and proprietary implementation for a DiffServ capable MIB exists.

The SNMP manager communicates with the SNMP agent through the SNMP protocol. The protocol supports three messages: (1) *get* with which the manager gets the scalar value of an object, (2) *put* with which the manager sets such a value, and (3) *trap*. The trap is not solicited by the manager. Instead, the agent triggers it in case a previously declared network event has happened at the device of the agent.

The Remote Monitoring (RMON) MIB

While the standard MIBs include objects to reflect the performance of networking interfaces (such as a byte counter, a lost packet counter, etc.) the RMON MIB [Wal95] defines management objects so that an agent can monitor the networking activity of a complete IP subnet. The RMON objects are arranged into the following groups:

The Ethernet Statistics Group. The Ethernet statistics group contains statistics measured by the probe for each monitored Ethernet interface on this device. In the future other groups will be defined for other media types including Token Ring and FDDI. These groups should follow the same model as the Ethernet statistics group.

The History Control Group. The history control group controls the periodic statistical sampling of data from various types of networks.

The Ethernet History Group. The Ethernet history group records periodic statistical samples from an Ethernet network and stores them for later retrieval. In the future, other groups will be defined for other media types including Token Ring and FDDI.

The Alarm Group. The alarm group periodically takes statistical samples from variables in the probe and compares them to previously configured thresholds. If the monitored variable crosses a threshold, an event is generated. A hysteresis mechanism is implemented to limit the generation of alarms. This group requires the implementation of the event group.

The Host Group. The host group contains statistics associated with each host discovered on the network. This group discovers hosts on the network by keeping a list of source and destination MAC Addresses seen in good packets promiscuously received from the network.

The HostTopN Group. The hostTopN group is used to prepare reports that describe the hosts that top a list ordered by one of their statistics. The available statistics are samples of one of their base statistics over an interval specified by the SNMP management station. Thus, these statistics are rate-based. The management station also selects how many such hosts are reported. This group requires the implementation of the host group.

The Matrix Group. The matrix group stores statistics for conversations between sets of two addresses. As the device detects a new conversation, it creates a new entry in its tables.

The Filter Group. The filter group allows packets to be matched by a filter equation. These matched packets form a data stream that may be captured or may generate events.

The Packet Capture Group. The Packet Capture group allows packets to be captured after they have flown through a channel. This group requires the implementation of the filter group.

The Event Group. The event group controls the generation and notification of events from this device.

The first version of RMON had some shortcomings. For example, the filtering cannot describe filters based on higher level protocols. So it was, for instance, not possible to distinguish between different TCP flows in order to derive statistics on the usage of web related protocols. Therefore, two years after RMON, RMON version 2 was standardized [Wal97] which can also distinguish between the application layer headers. Nevertheless, most devices do not even support the full RMON version 1 MIB. This is a good example of the lack of flexibility of SNMP compared to CSM.

Comparison to our Approach

SNMP is related to the CSM system since it provides network monitoring functionality. The RMON filtering and packet capture group could be used to implement a CSM T-component, since it provides the needed filtering and packet copy mechanism. Yet, most networking devices do not implement the RMON packet capture group. Traditional SNMP is not preferable to a customer-based service monitoring infrastructure. The mobile agent based CSM infrastructure has the following advantages over traditional SNMP:

1. SNMP is not flexible enough for customer-based service monitoring. Such monitoring must be tailored to each new IP service that a provider offers. Not all customers will be interested in the same measurement metrics. Therefore, huge MIB definitions would have to be specified. By the time the devices implement these MIBs and the provider has deployed these devices, the service may be out of date and the customer may have switched to another provider. With the CSM system either the provider, the customer or a third party supplier can rapidly develop a new measurement agent and distribute it.

2. The SNMP manager receives the network monitoring information through polling of all the SNMP agents. Since SNMP agents cannot preprocess the data, the monitoring data will use up significant bandwidth resources when transmitted to the manager. Furthermore, the manager that finally analyzes the measurement data may become a bottleneck. CSM agents can preprocess the monitoring data, thus putting it in a more compact form which only contains the information that is of interest. The CSM agent only informs the home application in case there is something relevant to be reported. SNMP can also emulate this behavior by using traps. However, traps are based on a simple threshold mechanism. Advanced schemes, such as random early notification (see section 4.5.1), cannot be implemented in SNMP.

3. The intent of SNMP is to provide a tool to the network operator of a domain. Therefore, fine-grained and user-based access control schemes are hard to implement in

SNMP. Either the customer has no access to the desired SNMP objects or the customer has access to SNMP objects that (s)he should better not have. The CSM infrastructure has a customer oriented security scheme.

4. SNMP does not provide topology support to the customer. While CSM agents can use routing and forwarding services of the CSM nodes, no such thing exists for SNMP. Therefore, each customer needs to find out on his/her own where the relevant SNMP agents are located.

6.2.3   Measurement Testbeds

Today, most large-scale network providers perform network measurements and monitoring, usually as part of a proprietary network management system (e.g. Cisco's Netflow [Cis00b]). Often, providers hesitate to make any results of these measurements publicly available, because they fear to offer attacking points to their competitors. This section presents two public and large-scale Internet measurements initiatives.

The NLANR Network Analysis Infrastructure

The National Laboratory for Applied Network Research (NLANR) is developing a Network Analysis Infrastructure (NAI) to support research on high performance Internet networks [MBB00]. The main focus is on passive collection of header traces, active measurements (based on ICMP), SNMP derived data, and Border Gateway Protocol (BGP) derived data. NLANR collects raw measurement data from the high-performance connection community in the United States. Various partners develop offline analysis tools for the data. Tools for the presentation and visualization of the data are also of interest.

OCXmon is the passive measurement sub-project of NLANR. Currently, 11 OC3/ATM monitors are deployed. An OCXmon monitor is a rack-mountable PC running the FreeBSD or Linux operating system. An optical splitter is used to connect the monitor cards of the PC to an OC3 or OC12 link. This is exactly the setting that the CSM T-component would need in order to accommodate backbone network speed. OCXmon thus shows that CSM T-components are even feasible without extending the router hardware. Further information on the OCXmon equipment is available at [NLA]. NLANR measurement data can be found on the world wide web at [DAT].

The PingER Project

The PingER project [MC00] performs active Internet performance monitoring for the HENP community. HENP (high energy nuclear and particle) physics experiments generate huge amounts[1] of data. The Internet is used to disseminate this data to universities all over the world. In order to assess the feasibility of the HENP networking goals, a

---

[1]During the whole lifetime of the project the expected data volume is somewhere between 10^{15} and 10^{18} bytes.

large end-to-end performance monitoring infrastructure is being set in place. The infrastructure consists of a network probing system along with a set of tools for analyzing the data. The architecture has become known as PingER, for Ping (see section 4.3.4) End-to-end Reporting. In regular intervals each site uses the Ping utility to send ICMP echo requests (pings) to a configured set of destinations. First, it sends 11 pings (of which the first is ignored) with a 100 byte payload, at 1 second intervals, followed by 10 pings with a 1000 byte payload also at 1 second intervals. In September 1999, 511 nodes in 54 countries participated in the measurements. The PingER analysis defines five metrics: packet loss, round-trip time, unreachability, quiescence, and unpredictability. The packet loss and round-trip time metrics are self-explanatory. The other three metrics need some further discussion. If no reply is received from all 10 ping packets, then the remote host is considered *unreachable*. For PingER it is extremely difficult to program analysis code to tell the difference between network related unreachability and a crashed end host. If the CSM infrastructure was used, then intermediary agents could help to locate the problem (see section 4.3.4).

If all 10 ping echoes return then the network is considered *quiescent* or non-busy. The frequency of this zero packet loss event may give clues of network usage patterns.

The unpredictability metric is derived from a calculation based on the variability of packet loss and round-trip time. If a path loses much more packets at one time than at other times or if the round-trip time fluctuates heavily between two measurements, then the calculation yields a high unpredictability value for this path. The unpredictability metric is a useful innovation of the PingER project.

The PingER methodology has some shortcomings. The measurements happen at regular intervals instead of Poisson distributed intervals. The PingER results may therefore be biased due to synchronization effects (see [PAMM98]). Furthermore, some routers treat ICMP packets differently than regular traffic. This may also bias the measurements since this means that the PingER measurements are not representative for regular traffic. Nevertheless, the collected data is useful to recognize short and long term networking trends and to identify network problems. For example, the deployment of the the TEN network (see section 6.1) had a measurable positive impact on the packet loss rate measured by European HENP partners. Also, university holidays have a measurable impact. Note that given the CSM infrastructure the ping listener agent (see section 4.3.4) can easily be adapted to provide a superset of the PingER measurements.

Comparison to our Approach

In academically influenced networks of the presented projects, network measurement data is often available via the Web or FTP. However, such data is too aggregated for customer-based service monitoring. It may only be useful as a CSM node service that provides access to aggregated measurement data. Then an agent can, for example, compare the throughput of the customer's traffic to the aggregated throughput of the whole network traffic. Architectures for fine-grained (per-packet) traffic data repositories have been proposed [KMKA99]. However, they do not collect the data on a per-service and per-customer basis. All collected data enters the same database. Therefore, they need to scramble the origin of the data for privacy reasons. This will also render the data useless for some customer-based service monitoring applications.

6.3   Mobile Agents for Network Management and Monitoring

This section discusses work closely related to the customer-based service monitoring infrastructure. In that work mobile code (mobile agents or active networking) is used for network management, or for network monitoring (a subtask of network management).

6.3.1   Network Management with Mobile Agents

The work in [BPW98] proposes mobile agents for various network management tasks and contains a detailed description of the advantages that the mobile agent paradigm offers:

- **Efficiency savings.** CPU consumption is limited, because a mobile agent executes only on one node at a time. Other nodes do not run an agent until needed.

- **Space savings.** Resource consumption is limited, because a mobile agent resides only on one node at a time and carries the required functionality along. In contrast, static multiple servers require duplication of functionality at every location.

- **Reduction in network traffic.** Code is very often smaller than the data that it processes, so the transfer of mobile agents to the sources of data creates less traffic than transferring the data. This is particularly true for CSM. All presented agents are relatively small compared to the monitored data stream. The largest and slowest agent is the VPN agent. It can monitor 3 Mbit per second and is about 30 KByte large (see section 5.2). Thus, the migration of the agent pays off after 0.08 seconds of monitoring at top speed. For smaller and faster agents the time to pay-off is even shorter.

- **Asynchronous autonomous interaction.** Mobile agents can be delegated to perform certain tasks even if the delegating entity does not remain active. For CSM this is interesting because a monitoring agent can still collect measurements when the home network is unreachable due to some network problems.

- **Interaction with real-time systems.** Installing a mobile agent close to a real-time system may prevent delays caused by network congestion.

- **Robustness and fault tolerance.** If a distributed system starts to malfunction, then mobile agents can be used to increase availability of certain services in the areas concerned. For example, the density of fault detecting or repairing agents can be increased. In the case of CSM this could be applied when the customer suspects that an agent or its results have been manipulated by a provider.

- **Support for heterogeneous environments.** Mobile agents are separated from the hosts by the mobility framework. If the framework is in place, agents can target any system. The costs of running, for example, a Java Virtual Machine (JVM) on a device are decreasing.

- **Online extensibility of services.** Mobile agents can be used to extend capabilities of applications, for example, providing services which allow to build systems that are extremely flexible.

- **Convenient development.** Creating distributed systems based on the mobile agents paradigm is relatively easy. The difficult part is the mobility framework, but when it is in place, then creating applications is facilitated.

- **Easy software upgrades.** A mobile agent can be exchanged virtually at will. In contrast, swapping functionality of servers is complicated. For CSM this is the often cited flexibility that the user has in deploying service tests.

6.3.2   The Script MIB

The IETF Distributed Management (DISMAN) working group recently standardized definitions of managed objects for the delegation of management scripts (the Script MIB) [LS99]. The script MIB will solve two pending problems of SNMP: (1) The processing and communication load on the central management station and (2) the overhead due to polling over distance. The script MIB allows the SNMP manager to send management scripts to devices that support the script MIB. The script MIB is programming language independent; any kind of executable code can be considered a script. The script MIB defines variables that encode the language support of the managed device. The Script MIB Extensibility protocol (SMX) [SQ99] can be used to separate language specific runtime systems (which execute the scripts) from the runtime system independent Script MIB implementations. A Java runtime system [SQK00] and a Perl runtime system [BG00] for the Script MIB exist. Both were used to address selected network management problems.

The Script MIB defines objects that allow the manager to carry out the following tasks using the SNMP protocol:

- Transfer of management scripts.

- Initializing, suspending, resuming, and termination management scripts.

- Transfer of arguments for management scripts.

- Monitoring and control of running management scripts.

- Transfer of results produced by management scripts.

Typically, a manager uses an SNMP *put* message to push the script to a device that implements the script MIB. An alternative is to put a URL into a dedicated variable which causes the SNMP agent to fetch the script itself. The manager uses the *put* message to set the command line arguments of the script. Later, the manager may use the *put* message to trigger the execution of the script as many times as desired. The script writes its results or termination code into appropriate SNMP variables. The SNMP agent can notify the manager that the script has produced a result by using SNMP traps. The manager can then use the SNMP *get* message to query the state and the result of the script.

In [QK99] the authors discuss applications of the Script MIB. They identify among other things that customers of QoS enhanced network services may want to measure and supervise the service level *themselves*. This is an important argument for CSM. The authors of the article used a Java script runtime system and their scripts were Java bytecode. They identified two shortcomings of the Script MIB: (1) The Java management 'scripts' are supposed to perform the SNMP interactions with the local devices. Therefore, the Java bytecode needs to carry an implementation of the SNMP protocol routines. This made the management scripts too large (about 500 KB). (2) The communication facilities of the Script MIB are very limited. Basically, the script can write one result into the appropriate SNMP variable[2].

Comparison to our Approach

With Script MIB support, the proposed customer-based service monitoring infrastructure can be built almost completely based on SNMP mechanisms. As mentioned in section 6.2.2, a device supporting the RMON MIB can play the role of the T-component. The node environment can be implemented as a Java runtime system attached to a Script MIB enabled device. An SNMP manager application can play the role of the CSM home application. Yet, such a solution has some shortcomings compared to a pure Java-based approach: (1) the aforementioned insufficient communication infrastructure offered to the management scripts. The CSM agents can communicate with the home application at will. The data format of CSM messages is not limited. (2) The transmission between the monitored device and the management script is a bottleneck. In an SNMP-based solution the management scripts must send SNMP *get* messages to fetch packets (polling). This is a critical overhead compared to the raw packet protocol (see section 3.2.2) which sends packets as soon as they are copied by the T-component. (3) SNMP does not provide topology support to the customer. The agents cannot be forwarded from one Script MIB to another.

6.3.3   Network Management with Active Networks

Active networks are a set of interconnected network nodes that not only forward data packets, but also interpret a subset of these packets as executable code and subsequently execute them (see section 2.2.1).

In [RS00] the authors propose a non-intrusive active networking approach for efficient distributed network management. Active packets (capsules) are send over ANEP compliant UDP packets. ANEP [ANE] specifies a mechanism for encapsulating active

---

[2]The script can actually write several results but each new result overwrites the old one.

network capsules for transmission over different media (here IP). In the proposed active networking based network management approach, the routers run a *diverter* which extracts ANEP packets and forwards them to the dedicated machine that provides an active engine (execution environment) to the capsules. The architecture is similar to the CSM infrastructure because it is non-intrusive and uses a dedicated machine to host the mobile code (capsules). Several capsules may belong to one distributed task (called a session). The capsules can either be sent directly to the router or they can be sent in a 'blind' way towards a destination address. Then, the first diverter on the way will reflect the capsule to its active engine. This is similar to the hop-by-hop forwarding in the CSM infrastructure (see section 2.4). The executing capsules contact the SNMP agent of the router to gather monitoring information or to reconfigure the router. The executable capsule contents consist of Java byte code. Security is achieved through the separation of the active engine from the router, through the Java security manager and through network utilization restrictions imposed on the sessions. Capsule authentication is also planned but not yet implemented.

The proposed active networking infrastructure can be used to implement a customer-based service monitoring system if the managed router implements an SNMP-based T-component (e.g. the full RMON MIB - see section 6.2.2).

However, the same drawbacks as described for the Script-MIB apply in that case: (1) Dependency of the available SNMP MIBs and (2) Inefficient packet copy forwarding (see 6.3.2). Furthermore, the topology support is limited. There is no such concept as the node services here. So the capsule cannot, for example, acquire topology information about the overlay network (where other active engines are located and to whom they belong). Another problem of the presented active networking approach is that large management programs may have to be split into several capsules. The rearrangement of these capsules has to be done by the active engine and is limited to 256 packets per session. Such a problem does not occur with CSM since the agents are transported on a TCP connection.

Nevertheless, the discussed work shows that a CSM infrastructure could also be deployed on a non-intrusive ANEP-based active network.

6.4 Open Issues

In this section we discuss unresolved problems concerning the proposed CSM infrastructure. We describe these issues and give some examples of related work that can help to fill the gaps.

6.4.1 Collaboration of Monitoring Agents

In the CSM infrastructure the home application receives all the results of CSM agents that it has sent. This book does not specify how the home application analyzes and interprets the results of the agents because this depends on the service being monitored. Nevertheless, there are generic high-level techniques to identify different failure situations in communication networks based on the input of several measurement stations. In

[LCL00] the authors describe methods to derive *codebooks*. A codebook is an optimal subset of events that must be monitored to distinguish the problems of interest from one another while ensuring the desired level of noise[3] tolerance. These methods are useful to develop and deploy a specific monitoring agent.

In the CSM infrastructure each agent performs monitoring for exactly one customer. One possible extension is that monitoring agents of the same or even of different customers may coordinate their actions and, for example, exchange results. The programmable coordination architecture for mobile agents MARS [CLZ00] proposes a shared and programmable tuple-space for inter-agent communication within a node. In CSM this could be implemented as a set of additional node services. Yet, the strong isolation of the CSM agents may break. Therefore, the CSM security model should then be extended, for instance, with MARS' access control lists.

Finally, we mentioned that the CSM agents report to the CSM home application. This scheme may not scale well for large customers. Instead, CSM agents should be able to report to yet another agent that may automate the reaction to certain monitored service conditions (e.g. automatic complaint to the provider or cancellation of the service). Such a scheme can be generalized so that CSM agents may form a reporting hierarchy of arbitrary depth.

6.4.2 Routing

The CSM nodes need access to the routing. With this information they can build up an overlay network and provide topology and forwarding services to the CSM agents (see section 2.4 and 3.7). The customer can use CSM query messages to find the ideal node for a given measurement or (s)he can forward the agent along a whole path. The CSM nodes thus need a way to fetch routing information. Such a mechanism may rely on the existing routing protocols like BGP [RL95].

The CSM nodes also need an internal routing mechanism that allows them to dynamically set up and manage their overlay network which is used to forward agents.

6.4.3 Artificial Intelligence

Distributed software agents are suitable for implementing computational models of artificial intelligence. Intelligence helps the agents to cope with unforeseen situations and enables them to act more autonomously. The presented CSM agents implement little intelligence. Instead, they are specialized for a well-defined monitoring job. Yet, CSM agent developers may develop agents which represent expert systems on a specific monitoring task. A CSM agent for network intrusion detection [BK98, JMKM99] is just one example.

---

[3]Erroneous event notifications: missing events or confusion between events.

Chapter 7

Summary and Conclusion

The Internet Engineering Task Force (IETF) has proposed extensions to the Internet protocol that address pending problems of today's Internet technology: quality-of-service support and security. The Differentiated Services (DiffServ) architecture (see section 1.2.3) allows network providers to offer quality-of-service guarantees to specially marked traffic classes. The security architecture for the Internet protocol (IPSec - see section 1.2.2) standardizes the use of tunneling and cryptographic mechanism for transparent per-packet privacy and authenticity of Internet communication. Both the DiffServ and the IPSec technology enable the Internet service providers to offer enhanced IP services and thus to generate additional revenues. Yet, the enhanced services introduce additional network management complexity, especially if several providers have to collaborate. Provider collaboration is necessary, for example, for end-to-end quality-of-service support because Internet traffic often travels through several provider networks.

This book addresses the following question:

- How can the correct operation of a multi-provider IP service be verified (by either the customer or the providers) in a dynamic, convincing, secure, and scalable way?

When Internet users request enhanced Internet services, such as DiffServ or VPNs, they should have a means to verify that the Internet service really is enhanced. This is a difficult task for several reasons: (1) Such services consist of per-packet actions and transformations that the provider performs *within the provider network*. (2) Traditional network monitoring provides only a small range of fixed metrics (e.g. throughput in bytes per second). The new IP services can only be verified by applying new metrics to the traffic. (3) The customer should not be able to abuse the service monitoring facilities.

In case several providers collaborate, a reliable and tamper-proof service monitoring facility becomes even more important. An ill-intended provider may participate in a service offering to obtain additional revenues but may not allocate the proper resources, since this generates cost. Both the customers of the service and the partner providers have an interest to identify such ill-intended providers.

This book proposes a customer-based service monitoring (CSM) infrastructure based on mobile agents. Using mobile agents for remote service monitoring is a novel approach. At their border routers the providers deploy non-intrusive execution environments (nodes) for the mobile agents. The agents are fully programmable and perform their measurements based on IP packet copies which are delivered to them by the node. The node implements security mechanisms that protect the node resources, protect the agents from each other, and ensure that the agents can only monitor traffic for which they have explicit permission.

Using mobile agents for CSM has several key advantages over stationary approaches:

- The customer's monitoring activity can take place within the provider networks.

- Mobile agents are programmable and easy to deploy and distribute. Thus, a new measurement metric for a new IP service is rapidly deployed.

- Mobile agents can perform their monitoring even when the customer is disconnected from the Internet and can thus, for example, further analyze potential connectivity problems.

- Mobile agents enable the customer to perform distributed tests in a flexible way. Measurements that originate from different locations can be correlated to identify a corrupted CSM node. CSM agents can dynamically roam to problem areas of the network where the number of measurement agents and increases, thus delivering a better picture of the service state.

- Mobile agent technology provides advanced security models and mechanisms.

In order to validate these advantages we implemented a CSM system. The CSM implementation (see chapter 3) introduces a number of new concepts:

- **T-components and filters.** The CSM agents calculate their results based on time-stamped IP packet copies. This guarantees the non-intrusiveness of the approach. The packet copies are generated by a specialized T-component which the agent cannot directly access. The agents have to request the copies from the CSM node. For that purpose they hand a filter object to the node that describes the desired IP packets. The node applies a second filter that describes the packets which the owner of the agent has access permissions to. This guarantees that the agent cannot monitor other customers' traffic.

- **Isolated execution environment.** The CSM node isolates each agent into a separate execution environment. Agent wrappers feed the agent with monitored packets stored in a queue. The agent holds only one object reference that merely allows the agent to deposit node service request objects. The agent wrapper manages the execution thread of the agent. The agent is thus effectively isolated from the rest of the node. On a Sparc ULTRA 5 a fast agent in an execution environment can handle up to 13'000 IP packets per second.

- **Lightweight resource control.** The architecture of the execution environment allows the CSM node to perform a lightweight resource control of CPU time, memory, and network traffic consumption. The control does not require bytecode rewriting or an enhanced virtual machine. For the CPU control, the agent wrappers account the execution time of the agent's packet handling method. A resource controller periodically checks if some agents' in-queues are filling up, and if so, which agent did make the least effective use of its CPU time. This agent is then terminated. The resource controller has only a minor impact on the performance. If the node is busy, the controller uses 5% of the node CPU time. For the memory control the Java object serialization mechanism is exploited.

- **Agent overload control.** Each agent has to implement a regular packet handling method and an emergency packet handling method. The latter is called when the agent in-queue is filling up. Thus, the agent is given a chance to get rid of the queued packets quickly thereby avoiding node congestion and subsequent termination of agents.

- **Flexible result delivery and display.** The CSM protocol provides a framework for agent developers that allows the agents to transmit monitoring results in arbitrary formats. The customer uses the home application to transmit agents and to display their results. The home application provides a display framework that permits the customer to display results in different ways (e.g. graphical or numerical).

Other features of the CSM implementation mainly exploit state-of-the-art technology (e.g. Java's class loader and the security manager) and well-known tools (UNIX scripting, PGP, and Tcpdump). Using a fast T-component (t-bone) the CSM implementation is able to monitor traffic at approximately 9 Mbps, the latency between the T-component and the agent is as low as 1 millisecond, the latency between the T-component and the customer-driven home application amounts to 55 milliseconds (for details see chapter 5).

The implemented CSM system allows the customers to develop new tests to verify the proper operation of the enhanced IP services. This book presents several examples of such tests, which cannot be performed with traditional systems (see also section 4).

- **Encryption verification.** One important innovation this book presents is the online cryptographic tests of the VPN traffic. These tests can reveal if due to error, misconfiguration, or ill-intention the VPN traffic is not or insufficiently encrypted. An inherent property of cryptographic mechanisms is that their output material has the same statistical properties as random data. The VPN control agent exploits this property. It uses the χ^2 statistics to define two randomness tests: the byte-frequency test that checks for uniform distribution and the run-length test that screens for independence within the data. Both tests can, for example, reveal if the VPN traffic is compressed instead of encrypted. Agent developers can easily create further (statistical) tests. None of todays static network monitoring tools can support such tests. If the tested data must first be delivered to a statistical test software that runs at the customer site, then this introduces huge networking overhead. If a VPN tunnel is monitored for two hours at a line speed of 1.544 Mbps (T1), then the customer must download 1.3 GByte of data to analyze it. With CSM, only a 30 KByte VPN agent must be uploaded. Note that the implemented agent can monitor the VPN traffic up to a speed of 3 Mbps (with limited loss up to 5 Mbps).

- **Customer-defined aggregation and separation of monitored traffic.** Traditional network monitoring tools have a fixed filter mechanism with which they aggregate or separate data (e.g. into counters). Thus, for example, the QBone project had problems determining whether DiffServ traffic was protected from regular traffic because not all monitoring devices could filter according to the DSCP byte. Furthermore, the SNMP RMON MIB had to be extended as it could not filter according to protocols of higher layers (e.g. HTTP). The CSM agents can program their own internal filters and, for example, implement meters that aggregate flows using the same DSCP value, or separate flows having the same endpoint addresses but using different DSCP values. Also, CSM agents can easily be programmed to analyze the higher protocol layers. Our ping measurement agent, for instance, analyzes the ICMP protocol to derive several measurements of performance metrics.

- **Localization of service problems.** Traditional end-to-end network management can identify problems but not localize them. The presented bottleneck bandwidth agent not only measures the bottleneck bandwidth between two communication endpoints. If the agent is deployed at several points in the network, then it can also locate the bottleneck link. Similarly, the one-way delay measurement agent and the round-trip delay measurement agent provide delay measurements of every intermediate part of the traffic path.

- **Protection from ill-intentioned providers.** Traditionally, the provider regularly (e.g. monthly) delivers a service performance report to the customer. Yet, it is easy for an ill-intended provider to forge such a report. It is much more difficult to forge measurement results when they are collected by the customers' mobile agents, because the provider does not know in advance the metrics as well as the time and location of the measurements. The customer can distribute agents with obfuscated code or nonsense agents to confuse the provider. In the future, mobile cryptography may become mature enough to protect the agent code. In addition, the customer can perform consistency checks by collecting different measurements at different locations, e.g. at the peering routers next to the provider to be tested.

We also implemented agents that calculate traditional measurement metrics such as: traffic loss, packet anomalies (broken packets or packets in wrong orders), throughput, one-way and round-trip delay, and jitter.

Outlook. A key strength of the CSM infrastructure is that customers, providers, and third party vendors can all develop monitoring agents. The CSM agents discussed in chapter 4 represent only a small subset of interesting monitoring applications. Further applications that can be deployed are:

- Customizable event notification that uses, for example, random-early detection or other heuristics instead of fixed thresholds.

- Trace-back of distributed denial-of-service attacks.

- Network intrusion detection.

Note that with each new IP service that is being introduced the number of interesting applications and thus the value of the CSM infrastructure increases.

A whole range of new CSM applications becomes available when the the CSM nodes offer further services to the agents:

- The injection of test traffic may become a node service. Then, the CSM agents can themselves perform active measurements from within the provider networks.

- An agent-to-agent communication service allows the CSM agents to exchange results within a CSM node. Result sharing means more effective use of the node resources and allows the customers to build agent hierarchies.

- A log file and management information base access node service can provide additional and preprocessed information to the CSM agents.

Finally, the CSM model could be extended from a non-intrusive monitoring model towards a full-fledged active networking model. Instead of working on IP packet copies, the CSM agents would have access to the original packet. They can thus control the packet forwarding and themselves perform packet transformations. Due to security, trust, and performance problems such an extension will probably not be deployed anytime soon. Section 4.5 describes the CSM node service and model extensions.

The presented CSM node implementation can handle a traffic rate of approximately 9 Mbps. It was tested on a real wide-area VPN tunnel and on a network of virtual routers. The throughput of the Tcpdump-based T-component is limited to 4 Mbps, which is mainly due to the fact that in our setting the limited network capacity between the T-component and the CSM node was shared with the test traffic. The performance limitation of the node is not so severe because the node usually only receives a subset (described by filters) of the complete network traffic. Nevertheless, the performance of the T-component needs to be improved when CSM nodes are to be deployed in the network backbone. Such high-performance T-components probably need specialized hardware.

When CSM is to be deployed Internet-wide, the implemented overlay routing mechanism (distance vector routing) may not scale. Then, integration of CSM node routing into the scalable two-tier Internet routing may be necessary. Moreover, a node advertisement and discovery mechanism would ease the customers' task to find the ideal node for an IP service test (see section 6.4 for more details).

Epilogue. In the future, Internet service providers will introduce IP services enhanced with a wide variety of quality features. The service monitoring infrastructure will be crucial to the success of such services because the customers can use them to build up trust in the services and verify that the services are worth the additional costs. Monitoring will also allow competent providers to deploy multi-provider services, while it can debunk providers with incompetent service management. We believe that the CSM infrastructure can improve the transparency of the IP service market and thus will play a crucial role in the Internet wide deployment of QoS enhanced services which will in turn increase the benefits of the Internet even further.

List of Figures

1.1 Overall scenario. 2
1.2 Virtual private network types. 4
1.3 The encapsulation security payload. 7
1.4 The authentication header. 8
1.5 Telecommunication management network model. 13
1.6 Life cycle of management processes. 13

2.1 Measuring at peering points. 22
2.2 The node environment. 23

3.1 Implementation overview. 30
3.2 The protocol object and the message objects. 36
3.3 The query and the agent execution protocol. 38
3.4 Node implementation overview. 43
3.5 Execution environment inheritance graph. 44
3.6 Execution environment. 46
3.7 Overview of policy, policy generators and user profiles. 51
3.8 Framework of the home application. 57
3.9 The CSM GUI and the agent sending form. 59
3.10 The query sending form. 60
3.11 The agent result display window. 61
3.12 The callback display window. 62
3.13 The visualization priciple. 63
3.14 Graphical representations of two packets. 64

4.1 Statistical test framework. 73
4.2 The histogram of byte values. 74
4.3 Real network bottleneck bandwidth measurement. 81
4.4 Distributed bottleneck bandwidth measurement. 82
4.5 The trigger application. 85
4.6 A measurement scenario with two virtual routers. 86
4.7 One-way delay between two virtual routers. 87
4.8 The ICMP echo request/reply packet. 88

4.9   Jitter measurement in a virtual router.   89
4.10   Measuring partial round-trip times.   90
4.11   Partial round-trip times of two virtual routers.   90
4.12   Round-trip times in uncongested network.   91
4.13   Round-trip times in mildly congested network.   92
4.14   Round-trip times in heavily congested network.   93
4.15   The three attacking targets.   95
4.16   A loss situation measured at honest provider sites.   98
4.17   Two agent input attack variants performed by provider B.   99

5.1   Influence of the packet generation rate.   107
5.2   Packet throughput of the execution environment.   108
5.3   Packet throughput of the execution environment.   109
5.4   Influence of the resource control.   110
5.5   Size dependency of the memory control duration.   111
5.6   Throughput of the execution environment including the TCP receiver. . .   112
5.7   Performance of the VPN agent.   114
5.8   Latency between the generation of a packet, its delivery to the agent, and
       customer notification.   117
5.9   The forwarding latency test setting.   118
5.10   T-component performance test scenario.   120
5.11   Latency of the Tcpdump-based T-component.   121

List of Tables

3.1 CSM communication layers. 33
3.2 CSM message objects. 35
3.3 User profiles. 50
3.4 The contacting information file structure. 65
3.5 The topology lookup file structure. 66
3.6 The use of the packages by the two installation variants. 68

4.1 Run test distribution. 75

5.1 Response times of the FastestAgent 115
5.2 Response times of the VPN agent 116
5.3 Response times 116
5.4 Forwarding latency over IAM 118
5.5 Forwarding latency over RVS 119
5.6 T-component load 120

List of Abbreviations

ACL	Agent Communication Language
AES	Advanced Encryption Standard
AF	Assured Forwarding
AH	Authentication Header
ANEP	Active Network Encapsulation Protocol
API	Application Program Interface
ASCII	American Standard Code for Information Interchange
ARM	Application Response Management
ASN.1	Abstract Syntax Notation 1
ATM	Asynchronous Transfer Mode
BB	Bandwidth Brokers
BGP	Border Gateway Protocol
BSP	Broker Signaling Protocol
CA	Certificate Authority
CPU	Central Processing Unit
CSM	Customer-based Service Monitoring
DES	Data Encryption Standard
DiffServ	Differentiated Services
DNS	Domain Name Lookup System
DoS	Denial-of-Service
DS	Differentiated Services
DSCP	Differentiated Services Code Point
EASE	Embedded Advanced Sampling Environment
ECB	Electronic Code Book
EF	Expedited Forwarding
ESP	Encapsulating Security Payload
FDDI	Fiber Distributed Data Interface
FIPA	Federation for Intelligent Physical Agents
FTP	File Transfer Protocol
GB	Giga-Bytes
GPS	Global Positioning System
GUI	Graphical User Interface

HENP	High Energy Nuclear and Particle
HTML	Hypertext Markup Language
HTTP	Hypertext Transfer Protocol
IANA	Internet Assigned Numbers Authority
ICMP	Internet Control Message Protocol
IDEA	International Data Encryption Algorithm
IEEE	Institute of Electrical and Electronics Engineers
IETF	Internet Engineering Task Force
IKE	Internet Key Exchange
IntServ	Integrated Services
IP	Internet Protocol (Version 4 or 6: IPv4, IPv6)
ISAKMP	Internet Security Association and Key Management Protocol
ISDN	Integrated Services Digital Network
ISO	International Organization for Standardization
ISP	Internet Service Provider
ITU	International Telephone Union
JNI	Java Native Interface
JVM	Java Virtual Machine
KB	Kilo-Bytes
MAC	Message Authentication Code
MB	Mega-Bytes
MD5	Message Digest 5
MIB	Management Information Base
MPLS	Multiprotocol Label Switching
MTU	Maximum Transmission Unit
NAI	Network Analysis Infrastructure
NLANR	National Laboratory for Applied Network Research
NSF	National Science Foundation
NTP	Network Time Protocol
OC	Optical Carrier
OSI	Open System Interconnection
PC	Personal Computer
PGP	Pretty Good Privacy
PHB	Per-Hop Behavior
PKI	Public Key Infrastructure
POP	Point-of-Presence
QoS	Quality-of-Service
QPS	QBone Premium Service
RFC	Request for Comments
RIP	Routing Information Protocol
RSA	Rivest, Shamir, and Adelman Algorithm
RTFM	Real-time Traffic Flow Measurement
RTT	Round-Trip Time

SA	Security Association
SLA	Service Level Agreement
SLS	Service Level Specifications
SMI	Structure of Management Information
SNF	Swiss National Science Foundation
SNMP	Simple Network Management Protocol
SPI	Security Parameter Index
SPO	Service Parameterization Object
SSH	Secure Shell
SWITCH	Swiss Academic & Research Network
TCP	Transmission Control Protocol
TMF	Telecommunications Management Forum
UDP	User Datagram Protocol
URL	Uniform Resource Locator
TMN	Telecommunications Management Network
VPN	Virtual Private Network
WAN	Wide Area Network
WWW	World Wide Web

Bibliography

[ABI]   Abilene. http://www.internet2.edu/abilene/home.html. Homepage.

[ANE]   Anep: Active network encapsulation protocol.
             http://www.cis.upenn.edu/~switchware/ANEP/. Homepage.

[ARM96]   Systems management: Application response measurement.
             http://www.opengroup.org/pubs/catalog/c807.htm, July 1996. Open Group
             Technical Standard C807.

[BB00]   Florian Baumgartner and Torsten Braun. Virtual routers: A novel approach
             for QoS performance evaluation. In *QofIS'2000*, September 2000.

[BBC+98]   S. Blake, D. Black, M. Carlson, E. Davies, Z. Wang, and W. Weiss. An
             architecture for differentiated services, 1998. RFC 2475.

[BBP88]   R. Braden, D. Borman, and C. Partridge. Computing the Internet checksum,
             September 1988. RFC 1071.

[BG00]   Luis F. Balbinot and Luciano P. Gaspary. Towards configuration man-
             agement of coralreef-based traffic measurement stations through the IETF
             script MIB. In *IEEE Workshop on IP-oriented Operations & Management
             (IPOM)*, September 2000.

[BGB01]   Roland Balmer, Manuel Günter, and Torsten Braun. Video streaming in a
             diffserv/IP multicast network. In *Workshop Advanced Internet Charging
             and QoS Technology of Informatik 2001*, 2001. to appear.

[BGK01]   T. Braun, M. Günter, and I. Khalil. Management of quality-of-service en-
             abled vpns. *IEEE Communications*, 39(5), May 2001.

[BGKL00]   T. Braun, M. Günter, I. Khalil, and L. Liu. Performance evaluation of a vir-
             tual private network. Technical Report CATI-IAM-DE-P-005-1.0, Institute
             for Computer Science and Applied Mathematics, March 2000.

[BGP97]   Mario Baldi, Silvano Gai, and Gian Pietro Picco. Exploiting code mobility
             in decentralized and flexible network management. In *Proceedings of the
             1st International Workshop on Mobile Agents*, Berlin, Germany, April 1997.

[BHV01]   W. Binder, J. Hulaas, and A. Villazon. Resource control in J-SEAL2. Technical Report No. 124, University of Geneva, January 2001.

[Bir]   Tina Bird. VPN information on the world wide web.
            http://kubarb.phsx.ukans.edu/~tbird/vpn/.

[BK98]   D.S. Bauer and M.E. Koblentz. NIDX: An expert system for real-time network intrusion detection. In *Proceedings of the Computer Networking Symposium*, pages 90–106, April 1998.

[BL94]   Michel Beaudouin-Lafon. *Object-oriented Languages: Basic principles and programming techniques*. Chapman & Hall, 1994.

[BLP00]   C. Bohoris, A. Liotta, and G. Pavlou. Software agent constrained mobility for network performance monitoring. In Harmen R. van As, editor, *Telecommunication Network Intelligence*, pages 367–387. IFIP, Kluwer Academic Publishers, September 2000.

[BMR99]   N. Brownlee, C. Mills, and G. Ruth. Traffic flow measurement: Architecture, October 1999. RFC 2722.

[BPW98]   Andrzej Bieszczad, Bernard Pagurek, and Tony White. Mobile agents for network management. *IEEE Communications Survey*, 1(1), 1998. Fourth Quarter.

[Bra97]   Jeffrey M. Bradshaw, editor. *Software Agents*. AAAI Press/The MIT Press, 1997.

[Bro00]   Marc Brogle. Active networking mit ANTS.
            http://www.brogle.com/marc/uni/ants/ants.php, March 2000.   Student project, University of Berne.

[Bud91]   Timothy A. Budd. *An Introduction to Object-Oriented Programming*. Addison-Wesley, 1991.

[Cab98]   Cabletron Systems, Inc. *6H202-24 and 6H252-17 SmartSwitch 6000 Interface Modules User's Guide*, 1998.

[CAN]   CANARIE. Canarie. http://www.canarie.ca/. Homepage.

[CBZS98]   K. Calvert, S. Bhattacharjee, E. Zegura, and J. Sterbenz. Directions in active networks. *IEEE Communications*, 36(10), October 1998.

[CC98]   Clyde F. Coombs and Catherine Ann Coombs, editors. *Communications Network Test & Measurement Handbook*. MacGraw-Hill, 1998.

[CER99]   Denial-of-service tools. http://www.cert.org/advisories/CA-1999-17.html, December 1999. Advisory CA-1999-17.

[CFSD90]   J. Case, M. Fedor, M. Schoffstall, and J. Davin. A simple network manage-
           ment protocol (SNMP), May 1990. RFC 1157.

[CHK97]   David Chess, Colin Harrison, and Aaron Kershenbaum. Mobile agents: Are
           they a good idea? In Jan Vitek and Christian Tschudin, editors, *Mobile Ob-
           ject Systems: Towards the Programmable Internet*, number 1222 in LNCS,
           pages 25–45. April 1997.

[Cis00a]   Cisco. *Monitoring the Router and Network*, 2000.
           http://www.cisco.com/univercd/cc/td/doc/product/software/ios120/-
           12cgcr/fun_c/fcprt3/fcmonitr.htm.

[Cis00b]   Cisco. Network management.
           http://www.cisco.com/univercd/cc/td/doc/product/rtrmgmt/, 2000.

[CLZ00]   G. Cabri, L. Leonardi, and F. Zambonelli. MARS: a programmable coor-
           dination architecture for mobile agents. *IEEE Internet Computing*, 4(4),
           July/August 2000.

[DAN]   DANTE. DANTE. http://www.dante.org.uk/. Homepage.

[DAT]   NLANR data cube. http://moat.nlanr.net/Datacube/. Homepage.

[Den00]   John S. Denker. Routing for linux-IPsec, 2000.
           http://www.quintillion.com/fdis/moat/ipsec+routing/.

[DH98]   S. Deering and R. Hinden. Internet protocol, version 6 (IPv6) specification,
           December 1998. RFC 2460.

[DS00]   Luca Deri and Stefano Suin. Effective traffic measurement using ntop. *IEEE
           Communications Magazine*, 38(5):138–143, May 2000.

[Fer00]   P. Ferguson. Denial of service (DoS) attack resources.
           http://www.denialinfo.com/, 2000.

[FH98a]   P. Ferguson and G. Huston. What is a VPN - part I. *The Internet Protocol
           Journal*, 1(1), 1998.

[FH98b]   P. Ferguson and G. Huston. What is a VPN - part II. *The Internet Protocol
           Journal*, 1(2), 1998.

[Fla96]   D. Flanagan. *Java in a Nutshell*. O' Reilly & Associates, Inc, 1996.

[Fre00]   Linux free s/wan project: Homepage.   Maillists & Archives, 2000.
           http://www.freeswan.org/.

[FS00]   P. Ferguson and D. Senie. Defeating denial of service attacks which employ
           IP source address spoofing, May 2000. RFC 2827.

[Fün98]   S. Fünfrocken. Transparent migration of Java-based mobile agents: Cap-
            turing and reestablishing the state of Java programs. In K. Rothermel and
            H. Fritz, editors, *Proc. Mobile Agents MA '98*, September 1998.

[GB00]   M. Günter and T. Braun. Internet service delivery control with mobile
            code. In Harmen R. van As, editor, *Telecommunication Network Intelli-
            gence*, pages 3–19. IFIP, Kluwer Academic Publishers, September 2000.

[GB01]   M. Günter and T. Braun. A fast and trend-sensitive function for the estima-
            tion of near-future data network traffic characteristics. In Bohdan Bodnar
            and Ariel Sharon, editors, *Proc. of the Applied Telecommunication Sympo-
            sium (ATS 2001)*, Simulation Series. The Society for Computer Simulation
            International, April 2001.

[GBB00]   M. Günter, M. Brogle, and T. Braun. Secure communication
            with active networks. Technical Report IAM-00-007, IAM, 2000.
            www.iam.unibe.ch/~rvs/publications/.

[GBB01]   M. Günter, M. Brogle, and T. Braun. Secure communication: a new ap-
            plication for active networks. In *International Conference on Networking
            (ICN'01)*, July 2001.

[GBK99]   M. Günter, T. Braun, and I. Khalil. An architecture for managing QoS-
            enabled VPNs over the Internet. In *Proceedings of the 24th Conference on
            Local Computer Networks LCN'99*, pages 122–131. IEEE Computer Soci-
            ety, October 1999.

[GHAM00]   B. Gleeson, J. Heinanen, G. Armitage, and A. Malis. A framework for IP
            based virtual private networks, February 2000. RFC 2764.

[Gra98]   R. S. Gray. Agent Tcl: A flexible and secure mobile-agent system. Technical
            report, Darhmouth College, 1998. PCS-TR98-327.

[Gün01]   Manuel Günter. *Managment of Multi-Provider Internet Services with Soft-
            ware Agents*. PhD thesis, University of Berne, June 2001.
            http://www.iam.unibe.ch/~mguenter/phd.html.

[Har97]   Elliotte R. Harold. *Java Network Programming*. O' Reilly, February 1997.

[HBWW99]   J. Heinanen, F. Baker, W. Weiss, and J. Wroclawski. Assured forwarding
            PHB group, June 1999. RFC 2597.

[HC98]   D. Harkins and D. Carrel. The Internet key exchange (IKE), November
            1998. RFC 2409.

[HGF+99]   J. Hulaas, L. Gannoune, J. Francioli, S. Chachkov, F. Schtz, and J. Harms.
            Electronic commerce of Internet domain names using mobile agents. In
            *Proceedings of the Second International Conference on Telecommunica-
            tions and Electronic Commerce (ICTEC'99)*, October 1999.

[Hoh]   Fritz Hohl.   The mobile agent list.   http://www.informatik.uni-
            stuttgart.de/ipvr/vs/projekte/mole/mal/mal.html.

[HSBR99]   S. Handelman, S. Stibler, N. Brownlee, and G. Ruth. RTFM: New attributes
            for traffic flow measurement, October 1999. RFC 2724.

[Int99]   Internet2 QoS Working Group. Qbone.
            http://www.internet2.edu/qos/qbone/, 1999.

[Ise97]   David Isenberg. Rise of the stupid network, 1997.
            http://www92.pair.com/camworld/stupid.html.

[IT]   "ITU-T". TMN management functions. ITU-T Recommendation M-3400.

[Jam01]   Thomas Jampen. Java API für PGP. http://www.cryptography.ch, April
            2001. Student project, University of Berne.

[JLM89]   V. Jacobson, C. Leres, and S. McCanne. Tcpdump. available via ftp to:
            ftp.ee.lbl.gov, June 1989.

[JMKM99]   W. Jansen, P. Mell, T. Karygiannis, and D. Marks. Applying mobile agents
            to intrusion detection and response. Technical report, National Institute of
            Standards and Technology, October 1999.

[JNP99]   V. Jacobson, K. Nichols, and K. Poduri. An expedited forwarding PHB,
            June 1999. RFC 2598.

[KA98a]   S. Kent and R. Atkinson. IP authentication header, November 1998. RFC
            2402.

[KA98b]   S. Kent and R. Atkinson. IP encapsulating security payload (ESP), Novem-
            ber 1998. RFC 2406.

[KA98c]   St. Kent and R. Atkinson. Security architecture for the Internet protocol,
            November 1998. RFC 2401.

[KBG00]   Ibrahim Khalil, Torsten Braun, and M. Günter. Implementation of a service
            broker for management of QoS enabled VPNs. In *IEEE Workshop on IP-
            oriented Operations & Management (IPOM'2000)*, September 2000.

[KMKA99]   Akira Kato, Jun Murai, Satoshi Katsuno, and Tohru Asami. An Internet
            traffic data repository: The architecture and the design policy. In *Proc. INET
            '99*, June 1999. http://www.isoc.org/inet99/proceedings/4h/4h_1.htm.

[Kna96]   Frederick Knabe. An overview of mobile agent programming. In *Analy-
            sis and Verification of Multiple-Agent Languages*, volume 1192 of *Lecture
            Notes in Computer Science*. Springer, June 1996. 5th LOMAPS Workshop.

[Knu81]   D. E. Knuth. *The art of computer programming*, volume 2 Seminumerical Algorithms. Addison-Wesley, 2 edition, 1981.

[Kra96]   H. Krawczyk. SKEME: a versatile secure key exchange. In *IEEE Proceedings of the Symposium on Network and Distributed Systems Security*, 1996.

[Lai92]   X. Lai. *On the Design and Security of Block Ciphers*, volume 1 of *ETH Series in Information Processing*. Hartung-Gorre Verlag, 1992.

[LCL00]   Chi-Chun Lo, Shing-Hong Chen, and Bon-Yeh Lin. Coding-based schemes for fault identification in communication networks. *International Journal of Network Management*, (10):157–164, 2000.

[Lea97]   Doug Lea. *Concurrent Programming in Java*. Addison-Wesley, January 1997.

[LO98]   Danny Lange and Mitsuru Oshima. *Programming and Deploying Java Mobile Agents with Aglets*. Addison-Wesley, 1998.

[LS99]   D. Levi and J. Schönwälder. Definitions of managed objects for the delegation of management scripts, May 1999. RFC 2592.

[Mac96]   Chuck MacManis.   The basics of java class loader.   JavaWorld, October 1996.   http://www.javaworld.com/javaworld/jw-10-1996/jw-10-indepth.html.

[MBB00]   Tony McGregor, Hans-Werner Braun, and Jeff Brown. The NLANR network analysis infrastructure. *IEEE Communications Magazine*, 38(5):122–128, May 2000.

[MC00]   Warren Matthews and Les Cottrell. The PingER project: Active Internet performance monitoring for the HENP community. *IEEE Communications Magazine*, 38(5):130–136, May 2000.

[Mil92]   David L. Mills. Network time protocol (version 3) specification, implementation and analysis, March 1992. RFC 1305.

[Mil00]   D. Milojicic. Applications of agent technology. http://www.iam.unibe.ch/~scg/AgentTechnology/, March 2000.   Spring School, Lenk.

[MJ93]   S. McCanne and V. Jacobson. The BSD packet filter: A new architecture for user-level packet capture. In *Proc. 1993 Winter USENIX conference*, 1993.

[MJ99]   Richard Murch and Tony Johnson. *Intelligent Software Agents*. Prentice Hall, 1999.

[Moc87a]   P. Mockapetris. Domain names - concepts and facilities, November 1987. RFC 1034.

[Moc87b]   P. Mockapetris. Domain names - implementation and specification, November 1987. RFC 1035.

[MSST98]   D. Maughhan, M. Schertler, M. Schneider, and J. Turner. Internet security association and key management protocl, November 1998. RFC 2408.

[NBBB98]   K. Nichols, S. Blake., F. Baker, and D. Black. Definition of the differentiated services field (DS field) in the IPv4 and IPv6 headers, December 1998. RFC 2474.

[NJZ99]   K. Nichols, V. Jacobson, and L. Zhang. A two-bit differentiated services architecture for the Internet, July 1999. RFC 2638.

[NLA]   NLANR measurement & operations analysis team. http://moat.nlanr.net/. Homepage.

[Orm98]   H. Orman. The oakley key determination protocl, November 1998. RFC 2412.

[PAMM98]   V. Paxson, G. Almes, J. Mahdavi, and M. Mathis. Framework for IP performance metrics, May 1998. RFC 2330.

[Pax97]   Vern Paxson. End-to-end Internet packet dynamics. In *Proc. SIGCOMM '97*, 1997.

[Pos81]   J. Postel. Internet control message protocol, September 1981. RFC 792.

[QK99]   Jürgen Quittek and Cornelia Kappler. Practical experiences with script MIB applications. *The Simple Times: The Quarterly Newsletter of SNMP Technology, Comment, and Event*, 7(2), November 1999. http://www.simple-times.org.

[Rab98]   Eddie Rabinovitch. Internet2 - your Internet connection. *IEEE Communications Magazine*, 36(3):17–18, March 1998.

[Riv92]   R. Rivest. The MD5 message-digest algorithm, April 1992. RFC 1321.

[RL95]   Y. Rekhter and T. Li. A border gateway protocol 4 (BGP-4), March 1995. RFC 1771.

[RMK$^+$96]   Y. Rekhter, B. Moskowitz, D. Karrenberg, G. J. de Groot, and E. Lear. Address allocation for private Internets, February 1996. RFC 1918.

[RS00]   Danny Raz and Yuval Shavitt. Active networks for efficient distributed network management. *IEEE Communications Magazine*, pages 138–143, March 2000.

[RSA78]   R. L. Rivest, A. Shamir, and L. M. Adleman. A method for obtaining digital
          signatures and public-key cryptosystems. *Communications of the ACM*,
          21(2):120–126, February 1978.

[SBB+00] N. Suri, J. M. Bradshaw, M. R. Breedy, P. T. Groth, G. A. Hill, and R. Jef-
          fers. Strong mobility and fine-grained resource control in NOMADS. In
          D. Kotz and F. Mattern, editors, *Agent Systems, Mobile Agents, and Appli-
          cations (ASAMA'00)*, number 1882 in Lecture Notes in Computer Science,
          pages 2–15. Springer, September 2000.

[SBBS01] G. Stattenberger, T. Braun, M. Brunner, and H. Stüttgen. Performance eval-
          uation of a diffserv linux implementation.
          http://www.iam.unibe.ch/~rvs/publications/, 2001. Submitted for publica-
          tion.

[Sch96]   B. Schneier. *Applied Cryptography*. John Wiley and Son, 1996.

[Sec00]   Securityfocus.com. VPN Maillist Archive, February 2000.
          http://www.securityfocus.com/.

[Sot00]   Juan Soto. Randomness testing of the AES candidate algorithms.
          http://csrc.nist.gov/encryption/aes/round1/r1-rand.pdf, 2000.

[SQ99]   J. Schönwälder and J. Quittek. Script MIB extensibility protocol version
          1.0, May 1999. RFC 2593.

[SQK00]   Jürgen Schönwälder, Jürgen Quittek, and Cornelia Kappler. Building dis-
          tributed management applications with the IETF script MIB. *IEEE Journal
          on Selected Areas in Communications*, 18(5), May 2000.

[ST98]   T. Sander and C. Tschudin. Towards mobile cryptography. In *Proceedings
          of the IEEE Symposium on Security and Privacy*, Oakland, CA, 1998. IEEE
          Computer Society Press.

[Sta99]   W. Stallings. *SNMP*. Addison-Wesley, third edition, 1999.

[Suna]   Sun Microsystems. Object serialization.
          http://java.sun.com/products/jdk/1.2/docs/guide/serialization/.

[Sunb]   Sun Microsystems. The source for java technology. http://java.sun.com/.

[Tei99]   Ben Teitelbaum. QBone architecture (v1.0). http://sss.advanced.org/arch/,
          August 1999.

[THD+99] B. Teitelbaum, S. Hares, L. Dunn, R. Neilson, V. Narayan, and F. Reich-
          meyer. Internet2 QBone: Building a testbed for differentiated services.
          IEEE Network, 13(5):8–16, September/October 1999.

[Tsc99]   C. Tschudin. Apoptosis - the programmed death of distributed services. In J. Vitek and C. Jensen, editors, *Secure Internet Programming - Security Issues for Mobile and Distributed Objects*, number 1603 in LNCS, pages 253–260. Springer, July 1999.

[Tsc00]   Christian Tschudin. Header hopping and packet mixers. In *Proceedings of the Ninth International Conference on Computer Communications and Networks (ICCCN'00)*, October 2000.

[TSS⁺97]   D. L. Tennenhouse, J. M. Smith, W. D. Sincoskie, D. J. Wetherall, and G. J. Minden. A survey of active network research. *IEEE Communications Magazine*, 35(1):80–86, January 1997.

[Tur36]   A. Turing. On computable numbers, with an application to the entscheidungsproblem. In *Proceedings London Mathematical Society*, volume 42 of *2*, pages 230–265, 1936.

[TWOZ99]   A. Terzis, L. Wang, J. Ogawa, and L. Zhang. A two-tier resource management model for the Internet. In *IEEE Global Internet'99*, December 1999.

[Uni]   University Corporation for Advanced Internet Development (UCAID). Internet2. http://www.internet2.edu/.

[Vaa00]   Sami Vaarala. Win2000 ike and 3des. IPSec Maillist Archive, May 2000. http://www.vpnc.org/ietf-ipsec/mail-archive/msg00808.html.

[VB99]   Jan Vitek and Ciaran Bryce. The JavaSeal mobile agent kernel. In *Proc. Symposium on Agent systems (ASA '99) and Applications and Symposium on Mobile Agents (MA '99)*, October 1999.

[vBN]   vBNS. Very high performance backbone network service + (vBNS+). http://www.vbns.net/. Homepage.

[Ver99]   Dinesh Verma. *Supporting Service Level Agreements on IP Networks*. MacMillan Technical Publishing, 1999.

[W2K00]   Export version of windows 2000 IPsec silently uses weaker encryption. SecuriTeam.com, May 2000. http://www.securiteam.com/windowsntfocus/Export_version_of_Windows_2000_IPsec_silently_uses_weaker_encryption.html.

[Wal95]   S. Waldbusser. Remote network monitoring management information base (RMON), February 1995. RFC 1757.

[Wal97]   S. Waldbusser. Remote network monitoring management information base version 2 using SMIv2, January 1997. RFC 2021.

[WGT98]   D. Wetherall, J. Guttag, and D. L. Tennenhouse. ANTS: A toolkit for build-
            ing and dynamically deploying network protocols. In *IEEE OPENARCH
            '98*, April 1998. San Francisco.

[Whi94]   James White. Telescript technology: The foundation for the electronic mar-
            ketplace. General Magic White Paper, 1994.

[WJ99]   Michael J. Wooldridge and Nicholas R. Jennings. Software engineering
            with agents: Pitfalls and pratfalls. *IEEE Internet Computing*, pages 20–27,
            May/June 1999.

[Zim01]   Phil Zimmermann. Pretty good privacy. http://www.pgpi.org/, 2001.